W9-ASA-151

Canada and
Collective Security

THE WASHINGTON PAPERS

... intended to meet the need for an authoritative, yet prompt, public appraisal of the major developments in world affairs.

Series Editors: Walter Laqueur; Amos A. Jordan

Associate Editors: William J. Taylor, Jr.; M. Jon Vondracek

Executive Editor: Jean C. Newsom

Managing Editor: Nancy B. Eddy

Editorial Assistant: Ann E. Ellsworth

President, CSIS: Amos A. Jordan

MANUSCRIPT SUBMISSION

The Washington Papers and Praeger Publishers welcome inquiries concerning manuscript submissions. Please include with your inquiry a curriculum vita, synopsis, table of contents, and estimated manuscript length. Submissions to *The Washington Papers* should be sent to: *The Washington Papers*; The Center for Strategic and International Studies; Georgetown University; 1800 K Street NW; Suite 400; Washington, DC 20006. Book proposals should be sent to Praeger Publishers; 521 Fifth Avenue; New York NY 10175.

UA
646.5
.C2
.J63

The Washington Papers/121

Canada and Collective Security

Odd Man Out

Joseph T. Jockel
Joel J. Sokolsky

Foreword by John G. H. Halstead

Published with The Center for
Strategic and International Studies
Georgetown University, Washington, D.C.

PRAEGER

New York
Westport, Connecticut
London

JAN 1 3 1988

475759

Library of Congress Cataloging-in-Publication Data

Jockel, Joseph T.
  Canada and collective security.

  (The Washington papers, ISSN 0278-937X; vol. XIV,
121)
  "Published with the Center for Strategic and
International Studies, Georgetown University,
Washington, D.C."
  "Praeger special studies. Praeger scientific."
  Bibliography: p.
  1. Canada – Military policy. 2. North Atlantic
Treaty Organization. I. Sokolsky, Joel J., 1953–   .
II. Georgetown University. Center for Strategic and International
Studies. III. Title. IV. Series: Washington papers ;
121.
UA646.5C2J63 1986   355′.0335′71   86-5041
ISBN 0-275-92217-0 (alk. paper)
ISBN 0-275-92218-9 (pbk. : alk. paper)

The *Washington Papers* are written under the auspices of The Center
for Strategic and International Studies (CSIS), Georgetown University,
and published with CSIS by Praeger Publishers. The views expressed in these
papers are those of the authors and not necessarily those of The Center.

Copyright © 1986 by The Center for Strategic and International Studies

All rights reserved. No portion of this book may be
reproduced, by any process or technique, without the
express written consent of the publisher.

Library of Congress Catalog Card Number: 86-5041
ISBN: 0-275-92217-0 cloth
ISBN: 0-275-92218-9 paper

First published in 1986

Praeger Publishers, 521 Fifth Avenue, New York, NY 10175
A division of Greenwood Press, Inc.

Printed in the United States of America

The paper used in this book complies with the Permanent
Paper Standard issued by the National Information Standards
Organization (Z39.48-1984).

10 9 8 7 6 5 4 3 2 1

Contents

Foreword

Geopolitically, Canada is in many ways in a unique position. It is the second largest country in the world in area and has the longest coastline, but, with a population of only 26 million, it is one of the most sparsely settled. It has as its sole neighbor the United States, roughly 10 times Canada in population and GNP and infinitely greater in terms of power. But Canada also has historic ties with Europe and wider interests around the world. It occupies a strategically important piece of real estate astride the most direct missile and bomber routes between the Soviet Union and the United States, and it is a rich treasure house of natural resources. Consequently Canada is highly vulnerable to the international environment and relies heavily on international trade and cooperation, negotiation, and conciliation for its prosperity and security.

In this situation it is easier to identify the objectives of a national security policy for Canada than to devise a defense policy to achieve them. A clear objective for Canada, as for any country, is to exercise control over its own territory and to defend it if necessary. But the defense of Canadian territory by Canadian forces alone is impossible, because the territory is too large, the population too small, and the threat nuclear. Beyond self-defense, the security imperatives in this nuclear age are reasonably clear: to prevent war and deter aggression; to maintain the democratic values and institutions Canada shares with others; and to promote verifiable arms control, the peaceful settlement of disputes, and the rule of law. These imply making a contribution to the political management of East-West relations as well as to the military measures necessary for defense and deterrence.

In trying to define a credible and practical defense policy, Canadians are faced with a paradox and a dilemma. The paradox is to be found in the fact that there is no discernible threat to Canada apart from the threat to North America as a whole. The dilemma arises out of the fact that North America is where Canadian security will be at risk if the U.S. nuclear deterrent fails, yet Europe is still the place where the global East-West balance is at stake. This problem has been the subject of a running debate in Canada over the years. For most Canadians there is no question of becoming neutral or of leaving their defense entirely to others; the only defense policy that makes sense is a policy of alliances. But the question is where Canada can best contribute – and how much.

Canada is the only member of NATO, apart from the United States, that contributes to the defense of North America as well as Western Europe and the North Atlantic. Canada became a founding member of NATO with the conviction, born of the experience of two world wars, that North American security and European security were indivisible, and with the vision, nurtured by Canada's transatlantic ties, of a more closely knit Atlantic community. In the Canadian view, this was an alliance for the defense of both Western Europe and North America. It was also more than a military alliance, recognizing the intimate relationship among defense, political stability, democratic values, and economic well-being. These aspirations found expression in Article 2 of the North Atlantic Treaty (the "Canadian article"), but they were not fully shared by Canada's allies.

In practice European defense and North American defense have been treated separately, and the economic dimensions of the transatlantic relationship have been treated separately from NATO defense questions. Moreover, with the movement toward European unity, transatlantic relations have become more and more compartmentalized and polarized – compartmentalized between those matters dealt with in NATO and those dealt with in the European Communities or between the European Communities and the United States, polarized between the United States on the one hand and the major European powers on the other. The result has been to foster the "two pillar" concept of NATO as an alliance between two mythical entities, "Europe" and "America." So it is that Canada has become increasingly "odd man out," North American but not American, a country whose economic power has not really counted in NATO because NATO is not concerned with economic matters, and whose military contribution, divided between NATO and NORAD, has never been enough to make much of a difference.

With Prime Minister Pierre Trudeau's coming to power in 1968 a watershed was reached in Canada's defense debate. All bets were off as a comprehensive review of Canadian foreign and defense policies was launched at a time when the end of the Cold War seemed to lessen the need for defense and Canadians were preoccupied with domestic issues. Many felt that NATO no longer filled any Canadian requirement and that Canada had no significant role to play there. In the event the long-standing policy of alliances was reaffirmed; Canada would stay in NATO and in Europe. But the government decided to downgrade the defense effort in general and the commitments in Europe in particular. The Canadian troops in West Germany were cut in half, the strength of the Canadian armed forces was reduced, and capital equipment expenditures were frozen.

Since then Canada has been living beyond its means, both economically and militarily. It has been accumulating an enormous budget deficit, which now amounts to almost twice the U.S. deficit in proportionate terms. It has allowed its military capabilities to run down to the point at which they can no longer meet the commitments. In the last five years Canada has begun to rebuild the armed forces and to correct the worst deficiencies, but years of neglect, the impact of technological change, and the steeply rising cost of military hardware have raised the price tag of modernization faster than the real increase in defense budgets. Meanwhile the commitments in North America, the North Atlantic, and Western Europe have remained undiminished. The chickens are now coming home to roost all at once. The gap between existing defense commitments and in-place capabilities has become dangerous just at a time when urgent action is called for to reduce the budget deficit and restore the economy in the wake of the recession.

When Prime Minister Brian Mulroney was elected in 1984, he announced his intention of doing more for defense and doing it in close cooperation with Canada's allies, especially the United States. He has given proof of his good intentions by concluding an agreement with the United States on the modernization of North American air defense and reinforcing Canadian troops in Europe. But he has also made it clear that, in view of the state of the economy, the objectives of a substantial real growth of defense expenditures and an increase in both regular and reserve forces cannot be achieved for the time being. And he has yet to show whether his government can set priorities and adjust commitments in a way that will close, or at least narrow, the commitment-capability gap.

Joseph Jockel and Joel Sokolsky have done a useful and timely service to Canada and the alliance by drawing attention to this gap. Their analysis of the military factors involved and the consequences for the effectiveness and credibility of Canada's defense effort deserve serious attention, as do their thought-provoking proposals to restructure the defense posture. Their analysis of economic and political factors is unlikely to further their cause, however. No democratic government can be expected to ignore the importance of a sound economic base for its defense effort. Nor can it be expected to ask its citizens to do more for the defense of its allies as well as themselves while holding out no prospect of their having any influence on alliance policies. And a sovereign government is unlikely to react well to a threat of "penalties" or "sanctions" if it does not restructure its defense posture along lines proposed from without. Apart from the fact that NATO does not work that way, it is not the way to deal with a sovereign and democratic government. The very suggestion of such a threat would be seen by other allies as setting a dangerous precedent and would have a totally counterproductive effect in Canada.

John G. H. Halstead
Former Canadian Ambassador to NATO
and the Federal Republic of Germany
Ottawa
March 1986

About the Authors

Joseph T. Jockel has been director of Canadian Studies at St. Lawrence University, Canton, New York since 1980. Prior to that he was on the faculty of the Center of Canadian Studies, The Johns Hopkins University School of Advanced International Studies, where he also earned his Ph.D. with a doctoral thesis on Canada and North American air defense. During the 1984–1985 academic year, Professor Jockel was a Council on Foreign Relations fellow at the U.S. State Department's Office of Canadian Affairs. In 1985 he took a NATO fellowship. An American citizen, he has written several articles on Canadian foreign and defense policy.

Joel J. Sokolsky is assistant professor at the Centre for Foreign Policy Studies, Dalhousie University, Halifax, Canada. He was formerly on the faculty of the Center of Canadian Studies, The Johns Hopkins University School of Advanced International Studies. He has recently completed a doctoral thesis on NATO maritime strategy at Harvard University and was a NATO fellow. A Canadian citizen, Professor Sokolsky has published several articles on Canadian foreign and defense policy, as well as naval affairs.

About the Author

Preface

More than a decade ago, in a paper commissioned for a study on the future of the Atlantic community, noted Canadian scholar and former diplomat John W. Holmes referred to Canada as the "odd man out." "Having no longer a very serious role to play in European or North American defense," Holmes observed, "Canada finds itself increasingly in a position . . . of functional neutralism." It was not that Canadians no longer believed in collective security, but that the "lack of a clear military role," along with "fundamental strategic realties" and a belief in détente, had persuaded them that they had "little to contribute besides their bare presence."[1]

In 1986 Canada is even more the odd man out. Yet with the waning of détente and the continued growth of Soviet military power, it is essential that Canada once again assume a clear military role in the collective defense of the West.

1

Odd Man Out:
The Sorry State of
Canada's Armed Forces

Geographically, Canada has always been the odd man out in Western collective security. As one of only two North American members of the North Atlantic Treaty Organization (NATO), its position differs significantly from that of the Europeans. Yet, not being a superpower and not having nuclear weapons, its situation is only marginally comparable to that of the United States, under whose nuclear umbrella it is sheltered. Because it is a smaller country in comparison with the United States, yet shares similar security interests on both sides of the Atlantic, Canada has long faced particular difficulties in determining its defense posture.

For well over a decade Ottawa has attempted to cope with those difficulties by shirking its fair share in the defense of the West and deploying insufficient forces on both continents, as well as at sea. As a result, the Western alliance has not had the benefit of what could be credible and meaningful Canadian military contributions. Canada is today taking almost a free ride on the backs of its U.S. and European allies. In addition to the moral failings of such an approach, Canada is failing to pursue forthrightly, through the commitment of conventional military forces commensurate with its resources, two of its own most fundamental interests: the deterrence of war, including intercontinental nuclear war, and the preservation of a free and prosperous Western Europe. Thus, morally and militarily, Canada has also become the West's odd man out.

With the coming to power of a new Progressive Conservative government in September 1984, Canadians have begun what may prove to be their first real debate in many years about their country's defense policy, although thus far that debate has been marked more by sharply partisan exchanges and confusion than by enlightened arguments. Hope is rapidly fading that the new government will prove much different than its immediate predecessors in the defense policy it pursues.

Events outside Canada are in part responsible for the sudden revival of interest in defense issues. Canada, in addition to its contribution to international peacekeeping forces, has nominally accepted two external defense obligations. The first is to NATO, of which it is a founding member and under whose aegis it has continuously stationed troops in Europe since the days of the Korean War. The second is to the North American Air Defense Command, renamed in 1981 the North American Aerospace Defense Command (NORAD), which was created by the United States and Canada in 1957 and which has operational control over both countries' continental air defense forces. NORAD's commander in chief, a U.S. Air Force general, reports to both National Defence Headquarters in Ottawa and the Pentagon. His deputy is a Canadian general officer, and their staff is integrated with officers from both countries.

Both NATO and NORAD are in the midst of change. NATO, with the trauma of the intermediate-range nuclear force (INF) deployment by and large behind it, has been examining its conventional forces with a view toward reinforcing them, thereby raising the nuclear threshold. It is also focusing on new tactical approaches, such as "deep strike," to cope with the Soviet threat on the central front in Europe. Both the renewed emphasis on conventional forces and the search for new tactical doctrines will have important implications for Canada's minimal standing contributions to the alliance's military forces. NORAD has already begun, with Canadian involvement, a long-overdue upgrading of its aging defenses against bombers and cruise missiles. Its radar systems are being overhauled, and new fighter aircraft are being deployed. As has now become evident in both the United States and Canada, NORAD is on the eve of still further and more dramatic changes. Many more of its surveillance and communications systems will eventually be space based.

In recognition of the growing military importance of space, the U.S. Department of Defense activated in the autumn of 1985 a Unified Space Command, reporting directly to the Joint Chiefs of Staff (JCS) and located at Colorado Springs, Colorado where NORAD has long been headquartered. NORAD's commander in chief was given another hat as commander of the new Space Command. Both Canada and the United States will be sorting out the future relationship between the Space Command and NORAD. Canada, for its part, will have to determine in which aspects of space-based defense it will want to participate. Those aspects could include not only communication and surveillance systems, but conceivably antisatellite weapon (ASAT) efforts as well as new defenses against ballistic missiles should President Ronald Reagan's Strategic Defense Initiative (SDI) research program bear fruit. The deployment of SDI defenses could also place a greater premium on antibomber efforts undertaken in Canadian airspace and from Canadian soil.

The prospect of involvement in ASAT and especially the SDI has already proved fiercely controversial in Canada and has come to dominate the debate over Canadian defense policy that emerged during 1985. This controversy over the relationship between the SDI and Canada's involvement in continental defense has intensified because the current NORAD agreement expires in May 1986. Although it is all but certain to be renewed, the Canadian government is under intense pressure, especially from the opposition parties in Parliament, to insert wording into the new agreement making it clear that Canada has no prior commitment to participate in any SDI system.

The realization has also grown within Canada that the country's armed forces had fallen into shambles during the years of Liberal Party government under Prime Minister Pierre Trudeau, who held power from 1968 through 1984 ex-

cept for a brief period in 1979–1980. Horror stories have
abounded of an air force whose aging airplanes have fallen
out of the sky, of a navy whose ships were tied up in port
for lack of fuel, and of a cold-climate army with no over-snow
vehicles and insufficient transport to get its troops to the
battle area swiftly.

The root of the problem is money, or rather, the shortage
of it. Since 1969 when the Trudeau government decreased
the size of the country's standing forces in Europe as part
of a reordering of defense priorities, Canada has not spent
more than 2.1 percent of its gross national product (GNP)
on national defense, with the exception of 1975 when it spent
2.2 percent. Spending dropped at one point in 1981 to 1.7
percent. For several years the capital budget was frozen,
forcing the military to retain rapidly aging major weapon
systems. Canada's 1984–1985 defense budget of C$8.767
billion (approximately U.S. $6.4 billion), the last prepared by
the Trudeau government, constituted a minuscule 2.1 percent of GNP – the lowest percentage of any NATO member
except tiny Luxembourg and Iceland, which has no armed
forces. These are hardly two countries with which Canada
is in the habit of comparing itself. After all, Canada is a proud
member of the industrialized Group of 7 summit partners and
is a country that in the past has described itself as a "middle power." It has been called by its current ambassador in
Washington a "large power" and by some Canadian scholars
a "principal power."

For the past few years Canada has met the annual goal
of 3 percent real increases in defense spending that the NATO
countries set for themselves at the Washington summit of
1978. Ottawa has sought to draw attention to that figure and
away from the more salient one related to percentage of the
GNP spent on defense. Three percent real increases are far
too low for a country only spending 2.1 percent of its GNP
on defense. What should have been in Canada's case a floor
has been treated almost as a ceiling. But Canada has by and
large been able to get by, especially now that most NATO
countries are not meeting the 3 percent goal, even though
all but the two smallest are spending proportionately far

more of their resources on their military establishments
than is Canada. The last minister of national defense in
the Trudeau government went so far as to make the claim
in the House of Commons that "Canada needs to take a back
seat to no one in terms of its NATO contributions." In reality, though, Canada is just barely on the bus – riding almost
free.

Canada is a country of 25 million people. The C$8.767
billion budget of Canada's Department of National Defence
supports a small, all-volunteer armed force of only 83,630,
which includes the army, navy, and air force. By way of comparison, the Netherlands, with a population of 15 million,
spends about 3 percent of its GNP to maintain a force of 103
thousand. In a cost-saving move, Canada unified its forces
in 1967, creating a single-service Canadian Armed Forces
under a single chief of the defense staff, with all personnel
wearing, to their considerable initial disgruntlement, the
same green uniform. The combat forces of the unified armed
forces are deployed in four organizations, all of which are
underfunded, understaffed, and underequipped:

● Maritime Command (MARCOM), successor to the
proud traditions of the Royal Canadian Navy, is headquartered in the port city of Halifax, Nova Scotia and is undoubtedly in the worst shape of all the Canadian Armed Forces.
To attempt antisubmarine efforts within NATO – Canada's
traditional area of naval expertise – MARCOM has a small,
makeshift operational force of some 20 destroyer frigates, 3
submarines, various support vessels, and 18 long-range patrol aircraft (LRPAs). All but four of the destroyers are facing imminent retirement, although several of the 16 obsolete
vessels are being temporarily kept afloat by dubious "life-
extension" measures.

In 1983 the government approved the construction of six
new "City-class" patrol frigates, a fraction of the number of
ships MARCOM had requested. Unless those six are augmented, Canada, the country with the longest coastline in
the world, will be left with a two-ocean navy of only 10 advanced surface vessels – several of which can normally be ex-

pected to be in port at any moment for repairs and resupply. Moreover, none of them is being equipped for operating in ice, despite the new challenges Canada may be facing in its Arctic waters from Soviet submarines.

The three conventional-powered Oberon submarines, of 1960s vintage, are also obsolete and are mainly of use as training vessels and mock targets, yet, for lack of anything better, MARCOM has been obliged to keep them at sea with a Submarine Operational Update Program (SOUP). Among the support vessels, there are no mine-sweeping platforms. That task will have to be performed by Canadian frogmen with unreliable hand-held sonar or by allied navies, if they can spare the vessels. The 18 Aurora LRPAs are, with respect to their ability to detect submarines, of NATO caliber, but are half the number MARCOM estimated were needed. Not surprisingly, one Canadian military commentator has despaired that MARCOM's "fleet is exhausted and past redemption."[2]

● Mobile Command, (commonly called the FMC*, the abbreviation of its French name, Force Mobile du Canada) the land element of the armed forces, has a force of 18,338 located in three brigades across Canada. Canadian troops are also serving in peacekeeping operations in the Middle East, and the FMC has the additional task of keeping in readiness troops that could be sent, should the need and opportunity arise, on new peacekeeping operations. That force is clearly insufficient for the NATO and non-NATO tasks assigned to it.

In the event of an emergency, the FMC would be called on to provide some reinforcements to Canadian Forces Europe (CFE). The FMC would be called on to dispatch a battalion to Europe, which would form part of the quick-reaction Allied Command Europe Mobile Force, Land [AMF(L)]. It would also assemble, largely from units of the 5e Groupe-

---

*In Canadian usage, abbreviations for military units such as "FMC" do not appear with the word "the" before them. In this paper, the American practice will be adopted.

Brigade du Canada, located in Quebec, the 4,000-man Canadian Air-Sea Transportable (CAST) Brigade Group and deploy it to northern Norway to help defend NATO's northern flank. As Norway does not allow any foreign troops to be stationed on its soil, the prompt arrival of the Canadians in the event of an emergency would constitute a most useful contribution to allied defense. But because Canada has insufficient airlift capability, most of the CAST Brigade Group's equipment would have to be transported in Norwegian merchant vessels, resulting in a transit time of about a month. (A limited amount of Canadian equipment has also been prepositioned in the Norwegian north.)

It is hard to concoct a scenario in which an advance warning of a Soviet attack would permit the Brigade Group and its equipment to reach Norway before the outbreak of hostilities. If war began before the Brigade Group were dispatched, it is even harder to imagine that it could successfully cross the war-torn North Atlantic and Norwegian Sea. If Canadian reinforcements were indeed sent off to Norway and West Germany, the FMC would be left with only about 3,000 regular troops in Canada to help civilian authorities maintain order.

The official excuse is that under such circumstances the Militia (the army reserve), nominally a force of 16 thousand, could be mobilized. But the Militia and other service reserves have been allowed to atrophy badly. As a Canadian Senate committee put it in a recent study of Canadian Armed Forces manpower, "there are serious questions about the current effectiveness of the reserves owing to years of neglect, shortages of equipment, inadequate training, uncertainty about roles and the absence of a mobilization plan." It is therefore easy to envisage a Canadian government, in the event of an impending or actual war in Europe, thinking long and hard before sending troops to reinforce NATO forces in Germany and Norway.

• Air Command (AIRCOM) is the successor to the Royal Canadian Air Force. It operates a small air transport fleet and provides maritime aircraft, most notably the Aurora LRPAs and Sea King helicopters that, for day-to-day operations, fall under the control of MARCOM, as well as tactical aircraft, that the FMC operationally controls. AIRCOM's most prominent role, however, is air defense. Its Fighter Group, headquartered in North Bay, Ontario, constitutes Canada's fighter contribution to NORAD. It would also be responsible for deploying to NATO's northern flank two squadrons of aircraft in the event of an emergency. Three of AIRCOM's squadrons are part of CFE. AIRCOM has been phasing out its ancient CF-101 Voodoo, CF-104 Starfighter, and CF-5 aircraft in favor of the new CF-18 (a version of the F-18) being bought from McDonnell Douglas.

The problem, though, is that AIRCOM's resources, similar to Canada's land and sea resources, cannot meet the country's extended commitments. The total inventory of CF-18s is only 138 aircraft. These have to be divided between training, NORAD duties, Germany, and, in the event of an emergency, NATO's northern flank. As many can be expected to be down for repair at any given moment, and, as attrition will take an inevitable toll, AIRCOM would be spread unbearably thinly. The government refused in 1985 to act on a recommendation of the Canadian Senate's Special Committee on National Defence to acquire additional CF-18 aircraft to cover that thinness.

● Canadian Forces Europe (CFE), located at Baden-Soellingen and Lahr in the Federal Republic of Germany, are Canada's standing commitment to NATO Europe and constitute the vestige of the larger standing force Canada maintained in Europe during the 1950s and 1960s until the Trudeau government decided, in 1969, to halve the Canadian presence. CFE consists principally of two units: 1 Canadian Air Group (1CAG), which will eventually be equipped with three CF-18 squadrons, totaling 54 aircraft, and 4 Canadian Mechanized Brigade Group (4CMBG), currently a force of 3,200, whose principal equipment is 77 German-built Leopard tanks, along with other armored personnel carriers.

Ottawa has taken several steps in recent years to strengthen the Canadian presence in Germany. The Trudeau government, after a partial change of heart about the value of CFE, authorized the purchase of the Leopards and CF-18s, while the government of Brian Mulroney announced in early 1985 that CFE troop strength will be increased by 1,200 and will be protected by a new low-level air defense system. Nonetheless, even after these enhancements, CFE still makes a minuscule contribution to the forces that the Supreme Allied Commander, Europe (SACEUR) would have at his disposal if war with the Warsaw Pact were to break out.

The 1CAG's 54 aircraft are part of NATO's overall attack-interceptor inventory of some 2,600 aircraft. The 4CMBG's 3,200 troops are part of NATO ground forces totaling more than 2 million. Its 77 Leopards are a tiny percentage of the NATO force of more than 20 thousand main battle tanks. Moreover, despite its status on the books as a standing contribution to NATO, CFE has been kept at a manning level of only about 60 percent of wartime levels, a condition that will only be partially alleviated by the addition of 1,200 troops. To bring CFE to war status, soldiers and air personnel would have to be flown in from Canada.

The problem with the Canadian Armed Forces, therefore, is not only that they are badly underfunded, underequipped, and undermanned but that they are stretched so thinly over so many roles that all of their contributions to collective security are, at the very best, militarily questionable tokens. To preserve a nominal presence in Germany and at sea and to maintain a nominal reinforcement role in NATO, Canada has retained all of the NATO and NORAD commitments it accepted in the 1950s — during which time it spent between 6 and 9 percent of the GNP on defense. Then, the Royal Canadian Air Force deployed 12 squadrons of interceptors in Europe and 9 in North America. The army's brigade group in Germany was almost twice its current size. The Royal Canadian Navy, which in 1945 had been the world's third largest navy, was a fleet of 129 ships, among them 40 major combat vessels, including an aircraft carrier. In 1985 there are astonishingly few Canadian ships, and these are aging badly. In North America, there are too few Canadian aircraft.

In Germany, Canadian air and land forces are too small to be seriously considered in the balance of power. In Norway, that the Canadians would ever arrive, much less arrive before the Soviets, is doubtful.

It bears observing, though, that the soldiers, sailors, and air personnel of the Canadian Armed Forces themselves constitute a highly professional force and are well respected in the United States and elsewhere in NATO. It seems at times, though, that they are far more respected outside Canada than within it. U.S. defense attachés serving in Ottawa are often taken aback by Canadians who simply dismiss their armed forces as a joke. Many of Canada's often demoralized military personnel still soldier on in the hope that their small and poorly equipped forces will constitute the core of expertise around which someday a Canadian government might decide to build more substantial forces. In the meantime, they make do with what they have and remain resigned to the political realities. Asked by a parliamentary committee whether he would feel better if he were in charge of larger and more effective forces, Lieutenant General C.H. Belzile, the FMC commander, replied that there was "no doubt that I would feel considerably better with larger forces. However, it is not my job to state so. It is a political decision and my job, as humbly as I can state it, is to click my heels and do the best I can with what I have."

The Mulroney Government and Defense: Going in a Circle

The election on September 4, 1984 of the Progressive Conservative government of Brian Mulroney offered hope to those in Canada and elsewhere in the alliance who were concerned about the state of the country's defenses. The political decision to revive the Canadian Armed Forces seemed at hand. During the summer campaign the Tories pledged to address the problems facing the Canadian Armed Forces. No one was more scathing than the Progressive Conservative leader himself in his attacks on what the Liberal government had done to Canada's defenses. As Mulroney told an Ontario radio audience,

> Pierre Trudeau and his Liberal pals have done the ultimate disservice to Canada by running down our armed forces to the point where we spend less per capita of GNP on our armed forces than any other country in the Western alliance with the exception of Luxembourg.
>
> This is unacceptable! This is a first-class country, and we're going to go first class in the area of conventional defence under a new Progressive Conservative government. We are not going to ask men and women to represent the honor of Canada in third-rate ships, in fourth-rate aircraft and in tanks that are 28 years old. We are going to do it first class – first class equipment, deployment capacity and first-class wages – those are the conditions under which they're going to represent Canada.
>
> And I think in doing that, then we've paid our own freight to NATO and to NORAD and we have the respect and trust of our allies. That enables us to make pretty substantial strides in the area of peace negotiations when we come to the table to talk.[3]

During the campaign the Conservative spokesperson on defense issues, Harvie André, a Member of Parliament (MP) from Calgary, called for the party to commit itself to real increases in the defense budget on the order of 6 percent a year for five years, thus doubling the rate of increases of the past several years. That specific amount did not make it into the party's 1984 program, but the program did call for a "strong and sustained political and financial commitment until the Canadian Armed Forces can meet the task of preserving our sovereignty and contributing to the collective security of the NATO alliance." The party also called for an immediate review of Canada's defense policy and pledged, if elected, to issue a white paper on defense that "would focus upon our defensive posture as well as recommending remedial action on key issues facing the Canadian Armed Forces." A defense white paper had not been issued in Canada since 1971, when the Trudeau government offered justifications for its downgrading of the country's defenses, including the halving of CFE and the eventual decrease in the size of the armed forces from 104 thousand to a low point of 78 thousand.

These were just two of the many promises the Progressive Conservatives made during the 1984 campaign. The Progressive Conservatives also pledged to cut the country's massive budget deficit while respecting the sanctity of social spending. As there was little talk of tax increases, this left some people skeptical as to where the Tories would be able to find the money to reverse the fortunes of the Canadian Armed Forces. But with the largest parliamentary majority in Canadian history – 211 out of 282 seats in the House of Commons – it seemed the Tories could do anything they pleased.

Upon taking office, Mulroney and his new government immediately took several steps that left the impression that they were serious about improving the country's defenses. The prime minister named Robert Coates, a Nova Scotian MP who was a former president of the party and member of its right wing, minister of national defence. In the Trudeau years, the national defence portfolio had been effectively relegated to the status of a junior ministership. Coates, however, was appointed by Mulroney to the powerful Cabinet Committee on Priorities and Planning (often called the "inner cabinet"), the first time a minister of national defence had held such a seat. The Cabinet Committee on Foreign and Defence Policy, which had been used at times to keep the Department of National Defence in check, was dissolved. Henceforth the Cabinet Committee on Priorities and Planning, chaired by the prime minister, would consider defense issues. Officials in the Department of National Defence and members of the Canadian Armed Forces were elated with the status of their new minister. At the same time, Canadian diplomats quietly passed the word on in Brussels, Washington, and in other NATO capitals that with the new government, Canada had turned the corner on defense.

The Mulroney government sought to underline further the new importance it was giving defense. Coates traveled to Washington in early October 1984, where he met with U.S. Secretary of Defense Caspar Weinberger and repeated the new government's pledges to enhance Canada's military establishment. Together Weinberger and Coates issued a communiqué emphasizing that there is "no real alternative over the next several years to continued high levels of investment by both countries in defense," although Coates carefully avoided naming any exact figures. Weinberger, for his part, promised to strengthen access to U.S. defense contracts for Canadian firms under the aegis of the Canada-U.S. Defense Development/Defense Production Sharing Arrangements, with a view toward redressing Canada's deficit in defense trade with the United States.

Back in Canada, Coates announced that distinctive uniforms for the three combat elements of the Canadian Armed Forces would soon be restored, a move that was particulary welcomed at MARCOM, many of whose sailors were embarrassed to appear in foreign ports wearing their green uniforms. And in the "Speech from the Throne," the formal statement of government policy opening the new session of Parliament, the government proclaimed that "Canada will once again play its full part in the defence systems of NATO. Only in this way do we earn the right to full consultation and participation in the policies of that alliance."

In keeping with its campaign promises, the government also announced that formal reviews of both foreign and defense policy would be undertaken. Each would consist of a three-step process. First, "green," or discussion, papers would be issued by early spring 1985. These would outline issues and pose hard questions. Second, the green papers would be considered by parliamentary committees, which would invite public comment and issue advisory reports. The government expressed the hope that the green papers would also occasion extensive public debate. Finally, white papers setting out new foreign and defense policies would be issued by the fall of 1985. Word soon leaked out in the Canadian defense and strategic studies communities that a well-known and well-respected defense analyst from outside the government had been retained by Coates to draft the defense green paper. The news was most encouraging.

Doubts surfaced about Tory intentions when, in a "mini-budget" presented in November that was interpreted as the first clear indication of the fiscal direction in which the government was to head, the minister of finance announced that C$154 million was being cut from the budget of the Department of National Defence. Although the amount was relatively small, it was a jarring note. The government explained that since the rate of inflation had decreased, the cut was not really a cut in the department's purchasing power. Off the record, however, the Tories passed the word that the cut was necessary to show that they were serious about deficit reduction and that no department's budget could be considered sacrosanct. Having once demonstrated their fiscal determination, the government would find it easier to raise defense expenditures when the real test came in the first full budget the new government was scheduled to present in the spring of 1985. These were all reassuring arguments. The cut was an early and unpleasant indication, however, of how hard the Tories would find the task of coming up with the money to meet their pledges.

After Coates resigned as minister of national defence in February 1985, in the wake of a scandal involving a visit to an unsavory nightclub, Prime Minister Mulroney, to underline the new importance he attached to the national defence portfolio, gave the position to the deputy prime minister, Erik H. Nielsen, an experienced parliamentarian, party stalwart, and influential member of the government.

The winter of 1984–1985 was filled with announcements of steps that the government was taking to strengthen Canada's defense posture:

• Shortly before the March 17 "Shamrock summit" between Mulroney and President Reagan, Nielsen announced that Canada and the United States had reached agreement on the modernization of the North American air defense system. The centerpiece would be the replacement in the high

Arctic of the nearly 30-year-old Distant Early Warning (DEW) line, which was no longer capable of detecting all forms of potentially hostile aircraft and cruise missiles. The new radar line, which would be called the "North Warning System," would consist of 13 long-range and 39 short-range stations. Sixty percent of the C$1.8 billion price tag was to be paid by the United States and 40 percent by Canada. Canada was to operate the North Warning System, as opposed to the DEW line, which had been entirely paid for by the United States and was being operated by a private U.S. firm under contract to the U.S. Department of Defense.

● Nielsen announced that CFE would be augmented by 1,200 men, bringing it closer, but not up to, war strength. He further announced that the AMF(L) and CAST commitments would be enhanced by ending the troubling "double-tasking" under which the battalion constituting Canada's AMF(L) commitment would have had to try eventually to join up with the CAST Brigade Group in Norway regardless of where the battalion was deployed. Henceforth, each commitment would stand alone, increasing, in effect, the Canadian reinforcement commitment by a battalion.

● Bidding was opened for low-level air defense equipment to be located with CFE and in Canada for use by the CAST Brigade Group. The absence of such defenses had created a serious vulnerability.

● It was confirmed that the government intended to test deploy, for the first time, the full CAST Brigade Group to Norway in 1986.

At the March 1985 summit in Quebec city, defense issues were prominent. The president and the prime minister celebrated the seeming turnaround in Canadian defense policy and what appeared to be their common views on defense spending. "We think," they said in a jointly issued declaration on international security, "it is essential to strengthen NATO's conventional capabilities and accordingly reiterate our determination to continue substantial real growth in expenditures." They pledged "to reinvigorate the defence and security partnership between the two countries," the agreement on North American air defense modernization being the most immediate symbol. President Reagan, in the spirit of the day, said in a televised address that he wanted "to thank publicly Prime Minister Mulroney and the Canadian people for your commitment to enhance your contribution to NATO's conventional forces and our overall defenses. Your deficit as a percentage of GNP is bigger than ours, but you understand that protecting freedom is government's primary responsibility, and we salute Canadian wisdom and Canadian courage."

That was the high point of the short-lived turnaround in the fortunes of the Canadian Armed Forces. Despite the long list of real, but still marginal, improvements in Canada's ability to undertake defense commitments that had been announced by the Mulroney government since it took office and despite the longer list of public promises, the real test of Canadian intentions would be how much more money for defense the Progressive Conservatives would be able to come up with in their 1985 spring budget. The answer was provided by Minister of Finance Michael Wilson in May. Had President Reagan spoken later, his tone would hardly have been so congratulatory. The May budget revealed that the Mulroney government would spend no more on the Canadian Armed Forces than the outgoing Liberals had intended to. In fact, they would even be spending slightly less. The Liberals had projected a 1985–1986 defense budget of C$9.533 billion; the actual Tory budget for that year, as announced by the minister of finance, was C$9.385 billion. This would once again, depending upon how measured, entail a real increase of 3 percent. But defense spending as a percentage of the GNP would not rise above 2.1 percent during 1985–1986. Nor would it in 1986–1987, according to the May 1985 budget projection. Moreover, the government's claims of having met the goal of 3 percent real increases are somewhat questionable, as the increases were measured not against the overall rise in inflation in Canada, nor against the rise in the cost of defense goods, but against the more dubious "gross national expenditures (GNE) deflator."

In fairness, it should be pointed out that the Department of National Defence did quite well when compared with other departments, many of which had their budgets squeezed as the Mulroney government sought to come to grips with the huge federal deficit through a combination of cuts and tax hikes. Within that context, the roughly 3 percent increase for the Defence Department could be described, as it was by some commentators, as a triumph for its minister. And Canadian officials were quick to revive the well-rehearsed refrain that Canada once again was going to meet its NATO goal. Indeed, it was going to meet that goal at a time when the U.S. Congress was attempting to hold the U.S. defense budget to no real growth. Ironically, that would put the United States, but not Canada, at odds with the joint commitment in the Quebec declaration "to continue substantial real growth in expenditures for defence." But, of course, the salient figure, away from which Ottawa again sought to draw attention, was the percentage of the GNP spent on defense. The Mulroney government, like the Trudeau government before it, had decided that Canada could continue to shirk its fair share. Canada would remain the odd man out. That the budgetary decisions of 1984 and 1985 were not temporary measures was confirmed in Wilson's deficit cutting budget of February 1986. Again, the Defence Department fared better than other departments. Real growth rates for 1986–1987, however, will be held to 2.75 percent and only 2 percent the following fiscal year. Expectations are that these increases will barely allow the forces to maintain the status quo and that planned reequipment programs will have to be either spread out over more years, delayed, or dropped entirely.

The budgetary trends of the Mulroney government meant that the planned review of defense policy, to be incorporated in the green paper/white paper process, would be all the more important. If large increases in defense spending were not to be available, it could only make sense to reconsider priorities carefully, given that the Canadian Armed Forces were overextended to the point at which all of their contributions to collective security had become questionable. The Department of National Defence would not be given anything near the amount of money needed to bring them all up to par.

Unfortunately, prospects for a thorough review faded throughout the first part of 1985. The defense green paper never appeared. Nielsen revealed that he preferred to go directly to the issuing of a white paper by the end of 1985. The government's reluctance to issue a green paper was partially because of the at times tumultuous debate that broke out in the House of Commons in December 1984 over Canada's possible involvement in the SDI, an experience that Nielsen and his cabinet colleagues were not eager to repeat. But word soon spread in Ottawa that the draft green paper prepared by the outside strategic consultant had also met with the minister's ire because it raised the very question of rationalization of commitments, that is, dropping some to concentrate on others.

Like the Trudeau government, the Mulroney cabinet was apparently afraid that dropping any defense commitment, even if undertaken in conjunction with the strengthening of other efforts, might be seen by its allies as a diminution of Canadian participation in collective defense. During its first year in office, it had rushed about, taking steps to strengthen marginally and thereby reconfirm all of the country's military roles. Shipbuilding continued. The modernization program for North American air defense was launched. The AMF(L) and CAST commitments were divided, and plans proceeded apace to test deploy the CAST Brigade Group. Twelve hundred men had been ordered to reinforce CFE, and the Quebec security declaration included the statement that "We attach great importance to our continuing commitment to station Canadian and United States forces in Europe." Low-level air defense equipment was also being ordered. What was left to review? But Canada still had too few planes to meet its North American and European commitments; too few ships under construction to stave off the further decline of MARCOM; too little air transport capability to make the CAST commitment viable; too few regular and reserve troops in Canada both to send to Europe and to maintain for home defense; and too few tanks, planes, and personnel in Germany to make anything more than a token contribution. The forces were still stretched too thinly.

Although far behind the original schedule, the minister of national defence said that he would still issue a white paper in 1986. It remains possible that the paper will incorporate a hard look at Canada's overextended defense obligations, especially now that the Canadian Armed Forces will remain badly underfunded. Indeed, the minister may well conclude that propping up all of Canada's military roles will be all but financially impossible. Several of Nielsen's senior advisers are known to favor dropping one or two roles to concentrate on others. Nielsen himself is not known for his willingness to discuss publicly government decisions before they are taken. So he may be preparing some real surprises. (The foreign policy green paper, which unlike its defense counterpart was issued during the spring of 1985, did hint cautiously at the need to set priorities in reconciling defense resources and commitments.)[4]

Undoubtedly, however, the Mulroney government, through its incremental improvements in virtually all of Canada's commitments to collective security, made a thorough review more difficult. The government in its first year in office came full circle on defense policy. It took power in September 1984 justifiably critical of what the Liberals had done to the armed forces, charging that the Trudeau government had not provided the armed forces with either adequate funding or a clear set of priorities. But thus far, the Mulroney administration has also provided neither. In fact, except on the rhetorical level, there has been little real difference between the defense policy of the Progressive Conservative government and the one pursued by Pierre Trudeau as he left office in mid-1984. The white paper will reveal whether the Tories will continue on that course or will sketch out a new and distinctive defense policy of their own.

Defense and Her Majesty's Loyal Opposition

It is hard not to summon up a measure of sympathy for the Progressive Conservative government in its shying away from an extensive national debate and review of the country's defense policy. For all their apparently good intentions concerning defense, the Tories are faced with a political environment characterized by an opposition in the House of Commons determined to seize upon Canada's defense relationship with the United States to embarrass the government, by a press that is not especially well equipped to discuss defense issues, and by both a press and public that have been too quick to adopt the notion of a special Canadian role in world affairs as a sort of righteous nuclear virgin with a vocation for promoting international disarmament.

The job of the opposition in parliamentary governments is to oppose. In Canada, that certainly is the case. Canada has one of the more rough and tumble parliamentary environments in the democratic world. Party discipline is tight by British standards, incredibly tight by U.S. standards. The battle lines between the government and opposition are clearly drawn, with very little room for conciliation. Moreover, unlike the more staid British House of Commons, ministers of the crown in Ottawa come into the Canadian House for daily question periods "cold," that is, without advance notice of the precise questions they are to be asked by the opposition, although they can pretty much surmise the topics beforehand. As the question period is now televised across the country on cable and clips of noteworthy moments appear on the evening news, the atmosphere tends to be intensely partisan and has been dubbed, with substantial justification, "the best show in town." The year 1985 was one of the most raucous in Canadian parliamentary history, and defense issues were a major source of contention. Faced with the crushing Progressive Conservative majority in the current House of Commons, the two opposition parties – the Liberals who were shattered and reduced to only 40 seats and the New Democratic party (NDP), a social democratic party with 31 seats – have had all the more reason to rely upon what is their most formidable political weapon: the chance to embarrass the government.

From that point of view, President Reagan's SDI research program was a godsend. Canada has long been sheltered under the U.S. nuclear umbrella, which is a major reason why Canadian governments have been able to avoid heavy defense expenditures. Living under the umbrella, Canadians have understandably developed their own particular forms of nuclear angst. Many Canadians are unhappy that geography has placed their fate in the hands of the U.S. president, possibly subjecting them to "annihilation without representation." A related worry is that Canada's continental air defense forces, what few it has, are linked through the joint NORAD command to the nuclear forces to the south, making them accessories of sorts and in some manner depriving Canada of the ability to pursue an independent foreign policy. (This worry is precisely the opposite of the European fear that an SDI system will "decouple" the U.S. strategic nuclear deterrent from European defense. Canadians worry that geography has coupled them too tightly.)

Another concern, which is to a large degree a vestige of World War II and early Cold War experiences with a strong U.S. military presence in the Canadian north, including along the DEW line, is that the United States will once again overrun Canada's underpopulated regions with defense installations, threatening Canadian sovereignty. The possibility that the United States might, if the SDI research program eventually bears fruit, deploy new antimissile defenses, strikes vaguely, but nonetheless deeply, at all those Canadian worries that lie close to the heart of the Canadian-U.S. military relationship. Many Canadians are worried that the SDI could trigger an arms race or increase the chances of a nuclear war that Canada, by reason of its proximity to the United States, could not hope to avoid. The United States might link NORAD and the Canadian forces in it to the SDI, with or without Canadian consent, associating Canada with a defensive system of which Canadians would not necessarily approve. They might also want Canada either to deploy new and vastly more expensive continental defense forces or to permit the deployment of new U.S. forces on Canadian territory. The issue has proved in Canada to be just as controversial and to provoke as much public hostility as did the INF deployments among the West Europeans. It is not inaccurate, therefore, to call the debate over the SDI "Canada's INF."

The Liberal and NDP opposition were quick during the first year of the Mulroney government to seize on those fears. The NDP has long cast a jaundiced eye on Canada's external military attachments and has retained in its party program a call for Canada to withdraw entirely from NATO. The Liberals, after the opening of Parliament in 1984, quickly adopted a stance fiercely critical of the strategic arms race in general, a stance that involved calls for a nuclear freeze and opposition to the SDI. As a result of a vigorous and prolonged offensive in the House of Commons, the two parties enjoyed a considerable measure of success in entering the emerging debate on Canadian defense and recasting it in terms of the relationship between the SDI and what the Progressive Conservatives were doing not only about defense policy, but also about U.S.-Canadian relations in general.

The Tories were sometimes caught off guard, such as when Secretary of State for External Affairs Joe Clark vehemently and repeatedly denied in the Commons that an invitation had been extended to Canada to participate in SDI research, only to learn, upon leaving the chamber, that such an invitation had indeed been transmitted several hours before to his colleague, Erik Nielsen, and to other NATO defense ministers by U.S. Secretary of Defense Weinberger. The manner in which Weinberger had sprung the invitations was also unfortunate. It seemed to make hollow the assertions of both the Mulroney government and the Reagan administration that, as part of their reinvigorated defense partnership, they had established a new consultative relationship. But even when the Tories were prepared, the ground had shifted, and they were faced with an extremely emotional issue upon which the public was ill-informed and that tended to overshadow their own approaches to defense.

The Progressive Conservatives themselves adopted a cautious, although not critical, attitude toward the SDI. Clark, speaking on behalf of the government, endorsed the "prudence" of the SDI research by the United States. The endorsement was warmly welcomed by the Reagan administration, although Clark specifically reserved judgment on the desirability of deploying new antiballistic missile systems and underlined the importance that Ottawa continued to attach to the U.S.-USSR Anti-ballistic Missile (ABM) Treaty. Later, a decision on whether to accept Weinberger's invitation to participate in the research program was put off for months while a special task force as well as a parliamentary committee studied not only strategic ramifications, but also the extent of economic and technological benefits should Canada participate. The prime minister finally announced in September 1985 that although his government would not be contributing any funds to SDI projects, individual Canadian firms would be free to bid for SDI contracts from the Pentagon.

But the opposition, which wanted Canada to immediately reject the Weinberger invitation and condemn the U.S. research program as leading to potentially destabilizing deployments, was often able to portray the Tories' cautious stance in terms of a cave-in to U.S. interests. "It is disturbing," Jean Chrétien, the Liberal foreign affairs critic and former secretary of state for external affairs, said in opening the attack, "for Canadians to realize that everything the Americans are asking of the Canadian Government is agreed to." The NDP and other Liberals would take up the refrain again and again. It was a charge to which the Tories were sensitive. Since taking office they had been decisively pursuing a policy of "refurbishing" the country's relationship with the United States, as the prime minister himself put it. This involved passing legislation to remove barriers to U.S. investment in Canada (barriers that the Liberals, when they were in power, had imposed with NDP support), exploring the possibilities of establishing a free or freer trading relationship with the United States, and giving the United States what the prime minister called "the benefit of the doubt" in global affairs. All of this was symbolized by the Shamrock summit, which was a celebration of not only the new harmony in Canadian-U.S. relations, but also of the good personal relationship between Mulroney and Reagan. But as the representative of the much smaller partner in the North American relationship, no Canadian government can afford to be labeled as subservient to the Yanks, particularly not in the sensitive area of political sovereignty and nuclear weaponry.

The announcement by Erik Nielsen of the Canadian-U.S. agreement on modernization of the North American air defense system led to the Liberals and the New Democrats devising the entirely spurious argument that the Mulroney government, either consciously or inadvertently, had brought into the SDI debate. In particular, opposition spokespersons repeatedly claimed, incorrectly, that the North Warning System was the first step toward inevitable SDI deployments in Canada. Government spokespersons were obliged to explain again and again in response to the opposition in the House that the North Warning System could detect only cruise missiles and aircraft and not ballistic missiles and the SDI was only a research program that might or might not yield results, which in turn might or might not lead to the actual deployment of new defenses against missiles.

But the government, worried that the public might not grasp the difference, also overreacted, claiming that there was no linkage whatsoever between the SDI and the North Warning System. In reality, however, if new antimissile systems were ever deployed, they would take their place, along with the North Warning System, as part of the North American continent's integrated defenses. In that sense, there was a link. But deploying the North Warning System was necessary even if the SDI were never to go forward, for the aging DEW line could no longer detect all forms of the air-breathing threats. Deterrence continues to rest partly upon the ability to detect hostile weapons approaching the continent. Discussions with the United States on replacing the DEW line had begun even before the president had hit upon the SDI concept.

The Liberals were quite aware of those facts because the North Warning negotiations with the United States had been opened and were well under way while the Liberals were still in power. With both sides staking out extreme positions there was ample disagreement, and the issue remained before the public for months, generating considerable confusion. In retrospect, it was a mistake for the U.S. and Canadian governments to call the improvements in radar the "North Warning System" instead of simply an upgrading of the old and familiar Distant Early Warning line, which is in essence what the North Warning System is. Apparently Pentagon officials felt that the project could better be sold to the Congress as essential to the defense of the United States if it did not bear the description "distant."

The press generated still more confusion during the debate. No major news organization in Canada has a full-time defense correspondent, and the press, along with Parliament and the public, has paid scant attention to Canadian defense policy for years. Suddenly, though, defense was a hot topic. The press scurried to cover, and in many cases simply to understand, defense issues – not always with success. The results were sometimes humorous. The *Calgary Herald*, for example, oblivious to the fact that the new North Warning System, like the DEW line before it, was designed to detect only aircraft, reported that "Suspected Soviet submarine intrusions and other foreign challenges to Canadian sovereignty in the far North, could become a thing of the past with the advent of the . . . North Warning System."[5]

Other press stories, complementing the charges made by the opposition in Parliament, hinted at dark doings by the U.S. and Canadian governments. *Maclean's*, the widely read Canadian equivalent of *Time* and *Newsweek*, splashed across its March 4, 1985 cover news of "The Secret Defence Plan." Inside the edition it warned that "An ominous Arctic shield," that is, the North Warning System and related improvements, "raises questions about Canada's future capability to make independent military decisions." Breathlessly, it went on to alert its readership that "*Maclean's* has learned that 12 secret 'arrangements' exist between Canada and the United States, dating from 1964, to provide Canadian landing facilities for the dispersal and recovery of American interceptor aircraft during a crisis or wartime."[6] *Maclean's* had in fact just learned what had been public knowledge since the mid-1950s. Even before the 1957 establishment of NORAD, Canada and the United States had entered into agreements to allow their fighter interceptors to enter each other's airspace and be redeployed at each other's air bases. NORAD itself had been created to provide a single commander who, along with an integrated binational chain of command, could take maximum advantage of those arrangements.

The agreements to modernize the North American air defense system, including the North Warning System, were signed during the Reagan-Mulroney summit in Quebec. During his major address there the president delivered a heartfelt appeal to the Canadian people for their support of the SDI research project, telling them that "the possibility of developing and sharing with you technology that could provide a security shield, and someday eliminate the threat of nuclear attack, is for us the most hopeful possibility of the nuclear age." Unfortunately, that statement, and the prime minister's repeating in the security declaration that his government found the SDI research "prudent," fueled suspicions that luring Canada into the SDI was the hidden agenda behind U.S.-Canadian relations and that the Tories were not telling the Canadian public the whole story. Those suspicions were still further intensified by Secretary of Defense Weinberger. During a television interview broadcast from the Quebec summit he said that, in the long run, deploying new antimissile systems in Canada was indeed a hypothetical possibility. U.S. and Canadian officials had to issue clarifications quickly, lest the happy mood of the summit be spoiled.

Into all of this came William Arkin of the Washington-based Institute for Policy Studies, an organization deeply

critical of U.S. defense policy. In carefully timed, and, in
Canada, widely reported releases, Arkin claimed to have
classified U.S. documents that, he said, contained plans
to deploy to Canada, in the event of an emergency, nuclear depth charges for antisubmarine warfare and nuclear-
weapon-carrying B-52 aircraft. The U.S. government was
caught in a uncomfortable bind. In keeping with long-
standing policy, it refused to comment on the authenticity
of the documents that Arkin claimed to possess. Similarly,
it declined to comment on the status of nuclear contigency
plans. It did stress, repeatedly, that no nuclear weapons
would ever be deployed to Canada without the permission
of the Canadian government. President Reagan himself reem-
phasized the point in an interview with *Maclean's*, published
right before the Mulroney-Reagan summit. "Over the years,"
he said, "NATO has worked out various defense plans designed to strengthen deterrence. But under these plans any
deployments would be carried out only—let me repeat only
with the prior agreement of the states involved."[7]

The Mulroney government emphasized that there were
no nuclear weapons in Canada, that there were no standing
agreements whereby such weapons might be stationed in
Canada, and that it was aware of no U.S. plans to deploy
nuclear weapons to Canada. That led to charges that the
United States had secret plans that it was keeping from Ottawa. When the Mulroney government categorically refused
to rule out the hypothetical possibility that it might one day
permit the United States, in an emergency, to deploy nuclear
weapons, it was charged with altering what many Canadians
thought was their country's "non-nuclear policy."

In this case too, confusion was rampant. Many Canadians discovered during 1985, to their dismay, that their
country was no nuclear virgin. After having participated with
the United States and the United Kingdom during World
War II in projects to develop an atomic bomb, Canada had
decided in the first few years after the war's end not to pro-
duce nuclear weapons, despite its ability to do so. It thus
became the first country to adopt a policy of nuclear non-

proliferation. After the Progressive Conservative government of John Diefenbaker was brought down over the issue, the newly elected Liberal government of Lester B. Pearson in 1963 agreed to honor commitments made by Diefenbaker and to equip Canada's continental air defense forces with the capability to use U.S. nuclear weapons in surface-to-air and air-to-air missiles. It also agreed to a nuclear capability for the army brigade group and air squadrons in Europe. The nuclear role in Europe was dropped in 1972 and the last of the nuclear weapons in Canada was removed in 1984, leading many Canadians to take satisfaction with what they saw as their country's restored nuclear purity.

Canada, nonetheless, is part of an alliance that relies on both conventional and nuclear deterrence. In North America, the chief role of Canadian air defense forces is to help protect the U.S. deterrent, whose existence deters attacks on Canada. In addition, 30 years ago it was announced that aircraft of the U.S. Strategic Air Command had been granted permission to overfly Canadian airspace, under certain highly regulated circumstances, a fact that many in the press and public rediscovered during 1985. At sea and in Europe Canadian forces are deployed in conjunction with allied forces that might use tactical nuclear weapons. Canada, for that reason, has a seat on NATO's Nuclear Planning Group. In short Canada's non-nuclear policy does not mean what a lot of Canadians thought it meant.

The memory of the "nuclear weapons crisis" of the early 1960s has remained controversial, perhaps even traumatic. The opposition and the government, with Mulroney taking an energetic part, found time in 1985 to trade insults over whose party had been more responsible for the acquisition of nuclear capability in 1963 — the Progressive Conservatives under Diefenbaker, who made the commitment to accept the weapons, or the Liberals under Pearson, who honored it. Mulroney, as a young man and aspiring Tory politician, was a protégé of sorts of John Diefenbaker. He may therefore be particularly conscious of the fact that Diefenbaker, who in 1958 held the largest parliamentary majority in Canadian history until Mulroney won an even larger one in 1984, was reduced to minority status in 1962 and then fell from power in 1963 largely as a result of defense issues. This may well contribute to a certain reluctance on Prime Minister Mulroney's part to grasp the nettle of defense that had so badly stung his mentor and predecessor.

By the time Parliament adjourned in the summer of 1985 defense issues had been argued about in the Commons, in the press, and by the public to an extent not witnessed since the fall of the Diefenbaker government 22 years earlier. There was, however, far more confusion than enlightenment. A real debate would have addressed the central problem of Canada's defense policy: the yawning gap between the country's military commitments and its capabilities. Such a debate would have included both a moral and a strategic component. Canadians could have addressed the dilemma inherent in their enjoying an almost cost-free defense alliance, while their allies carry substantial burdens. They would have had the opportunity to assess the relevance and utility of the various roles Canada has nominally accepted in Europe, at sea, and in North America.

Instead, in the intensely partisan environment of the Canadian House of Commons, the opposition mounted often spurious and emotion-laden attacks, which put the Mulroney government continually on the defensive while trying to defuse charges of nuclear sellout, hidden linkages to the SDI, and wholesale abandonment of Canadian sovereignty. The government, for its part, decided not to encourage another round of the same with the issuing of a green paper. And neither side was prepared to address squarely and directly the questions that remain as a result of Canada's abysmally low level of defense spending and hopelessly fragmented force posture.

The U.S. Dilemma: What to Do about NATO'S "Lost Lamb"

It is no secret north of the border that the Canadian Armed Forces are in a shambles. Books with such titles as *In Retreat: The Canadian Armed Forces in the Trudeau Years* and *True North, NOT Strong and Free*, wherein Canada is described as NATO's "lost lamb," and numerous newspaper articles similarly entitled have been published by Canadians. A committee of the Canadian Senate has for the past few years been issuing report after report on the state of the forces chronicling weakness after weakness. Senior military and naval officers, upon retiring from the armed forces, have gone public with horror stories. The Business Council on National Issues, which is composed of the chief executive officers of 150 major corporations, found in November 1984 that the "Canadian Armed Forces are incapable of fulfilling the tasks assigned to them, with the result that Canada is not meeting its alliance commitments" and that Canada " . . . is clearly failing to carry its fair share of the Western defense burden." The council called for real growth in the Canadian defense budget on the order of 6 percent for five years.[8]

While in opposition, Progressive Conservative politicans hammered away at defense inadequencies, and their leader, now the prime minister, called conditions "unacceptable" and "the ultimate disservice to Canada." And yet, after the heady first few months of the Mulroney government, hopes of a real turnaround have faded. For the moment there is no prospect that the money will be found to revitalize the forces and only limited prospects that the government will rationalize the forces' commitments.

As the leading nation in the Western alliance, and as the alliance member with the greatest stake in having other members do more for collective defense, the United States would clearly benefit from a Canadian decision to enhance its participation in NATO and North American air defense. U.S. officials have long been unhappy with – or at best glumly resigned to – the poor Canadian contributions. The United States largely sets the strategic context in both North America and in Europe, to which Canada must by and large, as an alliance partner, accommodate its defense policy. Yet the United States has little direct leverage over Ottawa when it comes to Canadian defense spending. If it did, Canada would today be spending much more than the 2.1 percent of its GNP.

This absence of U.S. leverage is ironic, for Canadians are continually asking themselves how they can affect U.S. defense policy, often with a view toward encouraging what Canadians believe to be a more realistic stance in strategic arms control negotiations. To be sure, senior U.S. officials have taken almost every occasion during the past few years in encounters with their Canadian counterparts to encourage them politely to do more. These sessions have included the four meetings a year Secretary of State George Shultz has had regularly with the Canadian Secretary of State for External Affairs Joe Clark.

But Canadians are especially touchy about pressure from their neighbor to the south. Most Canadians, and the Mulroney government in particular, are anxious to maintain good relations with the United States, particularly in the economic area. But any direct pressure from Washington is likely to elicit a nationalist reaction. Bowing to direct U.S. pressure to increase defenses would appear to undermine Canada's independence. Washington has been realistic about these Canadian sensitivities and has thus almost entirely avoided going beyond polite, private encouragement to Canadian officials to do more. In fact, the general absence of public criticism of Canada's defense efforts by senior U.S. officials can largely be explained by their understanding that such statements would be counterproductive.

The United States continues to have vivid reminders of the depth of Canadian sensitivity. When the U.S. ambassador in Ottawa, Paul Robinson, who recently completed his term in office, publicly chastised the Canadian government on the defense issue, torrents of criticism erupted from almost all quarters. Robinson soon dropped the subject. In 1983 the Canadian press reported that U.S. officials – who had been assured that they were speaking off the record – had told an academic conference meeting in New York on the subject of Canadian defense policy about U.S. unhappiness with the Canadian defense effort. Prime Minister Trudeau immediately lashed back, castigating "Pentagon pipsqueaks." At the Quebec summit President Reagan decided to try the opposite tactic by congratulating the Mulroney government on the preliminary steps it was taking to improve the country's forces. It seems to have worked no better than the critical approach.

Unlike its relationship with the European allies, the United States cannot threaten to reduce its commitments to Canadian security in the hope of eliciting a greater effort. "Uncoupling" is not a possibility. Geography, not the good will of the United States nor Canadian-U.S. friendship nor even common interests, has placed Canada under the protection of the U.S. nuclear deterrent. There are no "Nunn" amendments (such as the amendment designed to withdraw troops selectively from Europe) directed against Canada.

Despite the differences over the extent of the Canadian defense effort, relations between the defense establishments of the two countries remain close, indeed closer than with any other ally. The Permanent Joint Board on Defense, established in 1940, and the Military Cooperation Committee, meeting since 1946, provide a measure of oversight for the defense relationship. Service-to-service contacts are also close and extensive. This is especially the case between the two air forces, which share NORAD responsibilities, and with the two navies, which share in the protection of the sea approaches to North America and in securing the North Atlantic in conjunction with other NATO allies.

The United States is Canada's largest trading partner, taking more than 75 percent of Canada's exports. It also provides most of Canada's foreign investment. Linking Canadian performance in the defense area to trade and other economic ties is unlikely to work for the United States, however. As a rule, Canadian-U.S. relations are characterized by an absence of linkage politics. Washington could not move against Canada in the economic sphere without adversely affecting some U.S. interests or poisoning the overall economic relationship. That relationship is important to the United States, more important in fact than any other. Canada is the

primary trading partner of the United States. Canadians buy
from the United States twice as much as the United States'
next most important trading partner, Japan, and about the
same amount as is purchased by the entire European Community. Canada is also the primary country for U.S. foreign
investment.

Canada and the United States are involved in bilateral
Defense Development/Defense Production Sharing Arrangements (DD/DPSA). Under its terms Canadian defense contractors may compete on roughly the same footing with U.S. contractors in bidding for U.S. defense contracts, even for those
involving classified technology. These arrangements are extended to no other ally. At Quebec, the president and the
prime minister, in their declaration on international security, reaffirmed the arrangements. The Canadian government
maintains a sizable bureaucracy to foster defense sales to the
United States and has been pressing the U.S. government
to take steps that will help redress the deficit in the defense
trade that Canada is currently running with the United States.
In response, Secretary Weinberger dispatched a team of Department of Defense procurement experts on a cross-country
tour of Canada to brief Canadian contractors on how better
to win U.S. defense contracts. U.S. and Canadian officials
met throughout 1985 on the DD/DPSA in a follow-up to the
reaffirmations exchanged by the heads of government at
Quebec.

The DD/DPSA was established in the late 1950s and early 1960s as a means of helping Canada bear the burden of
defense at a time when Ottawa was spending more than 5
percent of the GNP on its military — a fact that is generally
overlooked in Canada. Because Canada has not kept up its
side of the bargain, it might be tempting, as well as completely legitimate, for the United States, far from reaffirming the
DD/DPSA and helping to address the imbalance, to ter-
minate the arrangements altogether. In the DD/DPSA
the linkage between economic and military interests is
natural. Using it as a source of leverage would not appear
to violate the "rules" of Canadian-U.S. relations, which pro-

scribe linkage across issue areas. Yet this stick too would be counterproductive. Canada will need the DD/DPSA if it is ever going to undertake a reequipping of its forces. The DD/DPSA also benefits the United States by giving it access to some competitive Canadian defense technology and by maintaining a defense industry in Canada that contributes to the overall North American defense industrialization base.

Finally, linkage of an unfortunate nature could still occur. At a time when protectionist pressures are on the rise in the United States and elsewhere and when Canada and the United States are on the eve of a new and far-reaching round of trade enhancement talks, which may even lead to some form of Canadian-U.S. free trade, putting new barriers to the flow of defense goods across the border would set an unfortunate precedent.

So the dilemma remains. Canadians and their government have not summoned up the will to reverse the decline in the Canadian Armed Forces. And a workable U.S. approach to elicit a greater defense effort from the Canadians remains elusive.

2

Canadian Defense Policy:
The Setting

It might appear that the present condition of Canada's armed forces is the result of indifference on the part of past Canadian governments, mainly the postwar Liberal regimes, to collective security. But, in reality, Canada has been one of the countries to support the idea of collective security most consistently. The Canadian and U.S. strategic outlooks have been largely complementary since 1945. From the need for strategic nuclear deterrent forces to the importance of local conventional defense along the NATO perimeter, Canada has rarely questioned the assumptions that have guided the Western alliance in its efforts to maintain the peace and secure the political independence of its members.

But it is one thing to support broad approaches to security and the necessity for certain collective measures and another to believe that Canada makes a difference to the shared goals of its allies by its material contribution to the common defense. Thus part of the explanation for the fragented state of the armed forces is Canada's view of its contribution, which implicitly and sometimes explicitly avoids any claim of strategic relevance.

What present and past Canadian governments have claimed is political relevance. Through its material contribution to collective security, Canada has sought to secure for itself influence over the strategic policies of its allies, especially the United States. By maintaining troops, planes, and tanks in Germany and ships at sea—even at token levels—Canada has believed that its voice in allied councils is listened to more intently. Canadian governments have also believed that their contributions to Western security support the whole range of Canadian foreign relations with their military allies, from economic links to questions of East-West détente and arms control. And, in the broader sense, these contributions have been regarded as appropriate for Canada because, while it has not claimed to be a major power, neither has it seen itself as an insignificant one. Canada regards itself as a rightful member of the Group of 7 leading industrial democracies. In this sense, membership in and contributions to the Western collective security system simply complement and reinforce the essentially global perspective Canadians have of the world and Canada's place in it.

The present state of Canada's defense posture can be attributed to all these factors, which have meshed together so well that it becomes evident that the condition of the armed forces is not the result of neglect, but of deliberate policy choices.

The Canadian Strategic Outlook

In the green paper on foreign policy, released in 1985 over the signature of Joe Clark, secretary of state for external affairs, the Progressive Conservative government succinctly set forth what Canada's broad strategic outlook has been for the past 40 years:

> The most direct threat to Canadian security derives from the Soviet Union's military capabilities and antipathy to our values and from the consequent distrust and competition between East and West.
>
> The principal threat to Canada has been from nuclear-

armed ballistic missiles, against which the only effective defence has been strategic deterrence.

. . . with the advent of new generations of Soviet bombers and of cruise missiles capable of being fired from bombers or submarines (threatening not only Canadian and American cities but also the nuclear forces of the United States upon which strategic deterrence depends), a major upgrading of joint Canadian-American air defence warning facilities has become necessary.

Europe remains the most critical military region in the world. It is where the line is drawn most graphically between East and West, it is where the task of deterring aggression must start. . . .

In the thirty years since it was founded, the NATO Alliance has successfully deterred aggression against its members and has consistently endeavoured to improve relations between East and West. . . . [9]

This approach to the international strategic environment is based upon more than the fatalism of a small power that happens to be located between two nuclear superpowers. Canada has held that the cause of a future world conflict would be some kind of Soviet aggression or threat of aggression. Ottawa has, on occasion, feared that overreaction on the part of Washington might lead to an unnecessary war. Yet, overall, Canada, like the United States, has tended to view Soviet policies as a threat to peace and stability.

Canada has supported the link between strategic deterrence and political independence for the European democracies. That is, Canada has held to the Churchillian view that while the Soviet Union may not want war, it certainly seeks the fruits of war. A militarily weak and politically disunited Europe would be easy prey for Soviet influence arising from the USSR's superior conventional military capabilities. For Canada, as for the United States, it is essential that not only must war in Europe be prevented by deterrence, but also that Soviet influence there be negated through adequate Western military might and cohesion. Canada draws its strategic perimeter along the iron curtain, because it regards a world in which Europe is dominated by a hostile power as one not conducive to Canadian interests.

For this reason Canada recognized that nuclear weapons provide the indispensable link between U.S. and European security, despite the uncertainties, ambiguities, and constant dilemmas that nuclear weapons evoke in the European context. Thus Canada has gone along with the deployment of generations of tactical and theater nuclear weapons in Europe, and it has continued to support the NATO position of not disavowing the first use of nuclear weapons in the event of a Warsaw Pact attack.

Ottawa also supports the strategy of flexible response, despite its well-known problems, and has been in favor of a continued buildup of NATO conventional forces to broaden the spectrum of deterrence and to raise the nuclear threshold. Although fully in favor of maintaining the link between U.S. strategic nuclear forces and the defense of Europe, Canada, because of its geographic position, has an interest in having NATO so postured that any war in Europe will be confined to Europe for as long as possible and preferably kept at the conventional or limited nuclear level. In this sense, the Canadian view is closer to that of the Americans than the Europeans.

But, unlike the United States, Canada is not a global power. Its security interests are almost exclusively confined to the North Atlantic region. Although anything the United States does anywhere in the world is of concern to Ottawa because it may lead to a confrontation with the Soviet Union, it is only in the North Atlantic region that Canada sees itself as having a role in international strategic matters. Canada is not, for example, involved in Pacific military relations and does not equate the security of Asian countries with its own in the same way it does the West European nations. Although thus limited in scope, Canadian security interests are fully complementary to those of the United States.

This does not mean that Ottawa has supported or will continue to support every U.S. foreign or defense policy. From the Korean War to Reagan policies in Latin America, Canada has made its disagreements known to Washington. On certain NATO matters, such as trade with the Soviet bloc, Ottawa's views are closer to those of the Europeans than the Americans. In strategic matters, Canada has generally held to the mutual assured destruction approach to nuclear defense, including support for continuing the ABM Treaty. There is thus some uneasiness in Canada over recent developments in U.S. strategic thinking, which stresses nuclear war-fighting or counterforce approaches to deterrence.

Although Canada has often argued its right to disagree with Washington, it has also been aware that if disagreement spreads significantly through the Western alliance, allied cohesion could be stretched to the breaking point, something Canada explicitly wishes to avoid. Allied cohesion fosters a transatlantic political environment in which Canada is spared from having to take sides in a major U.S.-European rift.

Deterrence and allied cohesion have given Canada a world in which the threat of war is far removed, thus allowing it to pursue its basic national goals: unity and economic growth. The first is largely dependent upon internal factors and has been more or less successful. The second is very much influenced by the state of the international economic system, relations among the industrial democracies in particular. Canada has a large external economic sector. Exports constitute nearly 28 percent of the Canadian GNP; imports account for a somewhat lesser, but still important, share of consumption. Changes in interest rates, in commodity prices, and in customs and nontariff barriers all have a significant impact on Canadian economic performance. Although strategic considerations do not have a direct and immediate influence upon international economic relations, the stability of the international system since 1945 has certainly provided a favorable environment in which Canada has been able to pursue its economic interests.

The Myth of the "Unmilitary" Country

Although past Canadian governments and most Canadians have long appreciated the importance of nuclear and collective defense to their national interests, it has been some time since there was a strong feeling that Canada's military contributions to collective deterrence made a difference in the overall balance of power.

In one sense, this feeling of military unimportance was a self-fulfilling prophecy. In 1969, Prime Minister Pierre Trudeau justified his decision to halve the size of Canada's European forces by "reminding" Canadians that "we're perhaps more the largest of the small powers than the smallest of the large powers." He noted the "magnificent recovery" of the European states, allowing them to provide more and more for their own conventional defense, and discounted fears that his reductions in the Canadian Armed Forces would have "profound international consequences." For many Canadians who came of age in the 1960s and 1970s, strategic irrelevance seemed to be the armed forces' distinguishing characteristic.

Canada, of course, does have a military heritage, although this has been all but forgotten except by those who lived it. In World Wars I and II, the still small and struggling country made a contribution to the allied causes out of all proportion to its size. And the Cold War was a period of significant Canadian contribution to collective defense. Despite the sorry state of the armed forces today, there remains at least a small measure of personal respect for the quality and professionalism of the men and women who serve and who have been forced to make do with third and fourth-class equipment.

The perception of military irrelevance has roots in a much older Canadian tradition, one that has taken on the dimensions of mythology. So influential is this myth, that a major study of Canada's military past could be confidently entitled, "The Military History of an Unmilitary People."

The myth is derived in part from Canada's historical experience. Canada has had no need of a large standing force to protect itself from invasion or to hold the country together. During the nineteenth century, Canadian security was guaranteed by its inclusion in the British Empire. Not that the United States had, since 1814, seriously contemplated fulfilling manifest destiny by seizing Canada, but the presence of the Royal Navy, a few Imperial troops in Canada, and an ill-maintained militia provided all the "deterrence" the young country felt it needed. By the beginning of the twentieth century, the already well-established Anglo-American entente removed still further the threat of invasion from the south — even during the heyday of U.S. imperialism. Canadians did fight for the British Empire, but they did so in the Sudan and in South Africa, not in Saskatchewan or southern Ontario.

When the empire faced its most serious challenge in Europe in 1914, Canada rallied and astounded itself and the world with its military prowess, in spite of British generalship. Yet this was followed by a rapid demobilization and a growing isolationism that included a reluctance to fight on new Imperial frontiers. Europe, however, was different. Even that avowed antimilitarist, Prime Minister William Lyon Mackenzie King, realized in September 1939 that Canada would be threatened if the Nazis conquered Europe and perhaps England. Thus Canada entered the war that month and fought for two long years before Pearl Harbor brought the United States into the global struggle. Again, Canada distinguished itself on the field of battle and, by the conclusion of the war, was one of the world's foremost military powers.

This time, demobilization was short-lived. In 1949, Canada took a leading role in the creation of NATO and in the summer of 1950, dispatched forces to fight on the Cold War's first hot frontier in Korea. During the following years the supposedly unmilitary Canadians, who had previously eschewed standing military forces in peacetime, created a military posture not only proportionate to its resources — taking as much as 9 percent of its GNP — but also one that was dedicated to transoceanic commitments. Moreover, as in the case of the world wars, this military buildup was accompanied by a perception that what Canada did counted – to itself and to its allies.

In sum, Canadian history is not that of an unmilitary people, if unmilitary is taken to mean a people who cannot maintain military forces to defend themselves or who will not seek out and participate in alliances with other nations who share a common threat.

What Canada has been, however, is a country whose security has always been linked to that of others and, in the case of Britain and the United States, to the security of the world's dominant powers. It is perhaps this association, rather than a lack of military history, that accounts for the strength and persistence of the myth. After all, even at its world war height, Canadian military power often fell into the shadow cast by the might of its allies. In the postwar era, there has been a tendency to draw some even more lopsided comparisons. What military effort can 25 million people make when compared with that of 220 million in the United States? What value can conventional forces have in the presence of thermonuclear weapons and arsenals that can destroy the world 10 times over? There are some real and compelling answers to these questions. But under these circumstances not only does comparison appear to depreciate the importance of the armed forces, it also tends to undermine their value as symbols of national identity. Canada performed magnificently in the world wars, but few regard them as Canada's wars, few pretend Canada was instrumental in wartime diplomacy, and few can point to any Canadians among the great allied leaders. In the Cold War, Canada accepted as a matter of necessity U.S. leadership of the West. Its armed forces were important for the security of Europe in the process of rebuilding, but essentially collective security was a U.S. show or a U.S.-European joint undertaking.

Thus the myth of an unmilitary people is, in part, like all national myths, an effort to somehow distinguish Canada from other countries. It is related to the seemingly never ending search for a true Canadian identity. And its persistence makes it difficult for Canadian governments, who may believe that their country can and should be making a better contribution to collective security, to arouse strong public support for such measures.

Canada: "Stern Daughter of the Voice of God"

Another manifestation of the myth of the unmilitary people is the approach many Canadians, and sometimes their leaders, have taken to questions of international conflict. The view has often been expressed that Canada's unmilitary people have a special and distinctive calling in this field, as well as being endowed with certain attributes, most especially an unmilitaristic national psyche, which makes Canada uniquely suited to play the role of peacemaker.

Since World War II, Canadian governments have recorded a respectable although by no means large number of successes in international mediation, most notably Lester Pearson's role as mediator during the 1956 Suez crisis. For his efforts, Pearson, who served as secretary of state for external affairs and later prime minister, was awarded the Nobel Peace Prize. Canada has unquestionably earned the claim of peacekeeper par excellence, having served in UN peacekeeping operations, on the Indochina commissions, and now, as a result of a decision taken by the Mulroney government, on the Multinational Force and Observers (MFO) in the Sinai. Its successes in peacekeeping, though, outnumber its successes in peacemaking by far, but many Canadians confuse the first-rate record in peacekeeping with the country's far more limited history of peacemaking.

Canada has, in fact, never brokered a peace treaty, even among those warring nations between whom its forces have been stationed as peacekeepers. Nearly 40 years have passed since Canadian soldiers took up positions along the Arab-Israeli borders, yet Canada plays all but no role in Middle East diplomacy. Ironically, the United States, the most important external military power in the region, has been the most successful in mediating between the Arabs and the Israelis.

Of course there is no reason to expect Canada to play a peacemaking role. In general, instances are rare in which external actors who are not major powers have been able to broker peace treaties. In the Middle East, in the Indo-Pakistani dispute, and, more recently, in Namibia, Canadian goodwill has not been able to persuade other countries to beat their swords into plowshares.

The myth of an unmilitary country has fostered the belief in an even more ambitious Canadian world role, that of nuclear disarmer. Canadian defense policy has been largely shaped to support the needs of NATO and NORAD, both fundamentally nuclear-based security arrangements. But as former Secretary of State Henry A. Kissinger observed of Canada, the country's "instinct in favor of the common defense" has often been in conflict "with the temptation to stay above the battle as a kind of international arbiter."[10]

Twenty years ago, another former U.S. secretary of state, with a rich background in dealing with Canadians on global issues, wrote scathingly of this temptation. Although Dean Acheson had for the most part enjoyed the support and cooperation of Canada as he and others sought to create a new world order, he identified a growing tendency among Canadians to assume that their country, not burdened with the many day-to-day tasks of a superpower nor sullied with the possession of strategic nuclear weapons, could take a more dispassionate and more ethically enlightened view of the world. "Canadians," he wrote, "feel about their moral superiority as the authors of the American Declaration of Independence did almost two hundred years ago: 'We hold these truths to be self-evident!'" In world affairs, Canada saw itself, as Acheson acerbically put it, quoting Wordsworth, as the "stern daughter of the voice of God."[11]

If anything, this trend has continued since Acheson's day, more particularly in recent years. For example, parliamentarians, peace activists, and editorialists alike have frequently called on the Mulroney government to preserve what is called "Canada's traditional role as honest broker between the superpowers." No such role ever existed for Canada – or for any other nonsuperpower. Yet despite the complete lack of any evidence to support the claim, some in Canada write glowingly of this tradition, revealing by their account of Canadian efforts that there is no tangible evidence of this tradition. Thus a well-known Canadian arms control advocate could proudly record Canada's participation in one UN disarmament conference: "In general, the session may be regarded as a constructive, but not particularly productive follow up of UNSSOD, except, perhaps in terms of the number of resolutions adopted!"[12]

To a large extent, the perpetuation of this imaginary tradition of success has resulted from confusion between real influence on arms control and simple posturing. Thus the Legislative Assembly of Manitoba this year declared the province a "nuclear free zone," an action having no legal or other practical effect, largely in hopes of influencing U.S. policy. Other jurisdictions in Canada may be following suit. As one Manitoba political leader put it, "Much as a family member tells his or her loved ones when they have gone astray, we have a responsibility to exercise a moderating force on American policy when it becomes extreme and dogmatic." This is a peculiar idea, given the traditional, and largely justifiable, Canadian lament that the U.S. public pays no attention to developments in Canada. U.S. citizens could probably not say with any degree of certainty what precisely Manitoba is or where it might be located. The Reagan administration, which pays far more attention to Canadian-U.S. relations than it generally has been given credit for, is, on the other hand, not going to be swayed in its defense and arms control policies by such posturing.

Every country deserves to enjoy its national equivalent of Fourth of July oratory, and certainly U.S. citizens are in no position to criticize other countries for developing over-inflated national self-perceptions or even for a tendency to moralize. Perhaps, as well, no country is more deserving of U.S. indulgence on this score than Canada, whose at times fragile sense of national identity is threatened by linguistic and regional divisiveness and by the pervasiveness of U.S. culture pouring across the border. Canada's "special vocation" in world affairs is attractive to Canadians not only as a source of national unity, but also to the extent that it emphasizes such features as the search for nuclear disarmament, as a source of distinctiveness from the United States. Americans are soldiers; Canadians are peacemakers or "peacemongers," or at least peacekeeping soldiers. Americans build arms, especially nuclear arms; Canadians contribute to disarmament talks in New York and Geneva. Or so the myth goes.

This is not to say that there is no role for Canada in international arms control efforts. Quite the contrary, Canada's diplomats are probably more in tune with the realities of these efforts than the Canadian public is aware. The point of entry is its alliance relationship with the United States, in particular its NATO membership. Because the United States has consulted with its allies and informed them about the progress of U.S.-USSR arms control negotiations, Ottawa has had the opportunity to make its views known directly to the senior officials responsible for U.S. national security policy. U.S. negotiators or their appointed representatives often visit the Canadian capital to brief the prime minister and other officials.

This participation does not afford Canada any special influence over U.S. arms control decisions and, of course, over Soviet decisions. The views of the European countries, especially those upon whose soil certain weapon systems are to be deployed, carry more weight with Washington than Canada's views do. Nevertheless, Canada can, through its alliance participation, support the kinds of allied consensus on arms control that Washington is compelled to take into account. The classic example of this came with the decision to extend adherence to the unratified SALT II Treaty—an important arms control issue. Canada supported continued adherence, as did all the other allies, and Canada was able to join with these others in a successful effort to influence the president. This approach is far more useful than having senior diplomats call for arms control from the podium of some UN-sponsored gathering.

Problems arise when the myth overtakes the more subdued, yet ultimately more effective, alliance-oriented approach to arms control. Such was the case with the Trudeau "peace initiative" launched in the late fall of 1983. The prime minister was convinced that U.S.-Soviet arms control negotiations were going nowhere and that the world was moving quickly toward a serious crisis in East-West relations, if not to war itself. In Europe, tensions were high over the coming deployment of nuclear-armed cruise and Pershing II missiles, which were the subject of ongoing negotiations. Canada had supported the December 1979 NATO two-track decision to deploy and to negotiate, and the Trudeau government was not backing away from this support. Nor was the government willing to give into demands voiced by a number of groups in Canada that the testing of unarmed U.S. air-launched cruise missiles in western Canada be halted. Nevertheless, so persuaded was the prime minister that something had to be done that he called for a new approach to arms control, dubbing it the "third track," and went on a world tour to convince friend and foe alike that they had to be more serious about arms control. Trudeau was politely, if somewhat uncomprehendingly, received in allied capitals, including Washington, where President Reagan wished him "Godspeed." His reception in Moscow was less than enthusiastic. To Trudeau's mild displeasure, he did receive an extremely warm welcome in East Germany, whose leader took the opportunity to castigate the United States and thank the Canadian prime minister for calling the world's attention to the lack of U.S. concern for arms control.

Throughout the short-lived initiative, Trudeau declared Canada's continued allegiance to NATO and the principle of collective security. But it was clear elsewhere if not in Ottawa that he was undermining allied solidarity. What NATO needed, with the impending Soviet walkout from the INF talks as a result of the decision to deploy, was a united front. It is ironic that the Europeans who were to receive the new missiles maintained a measure of solidarity with Washington that few had expected, while Canada, for which the INF deployment caused no internal political problems, appeared out of step with its allies. For no matter how much Trudeau claimed to be supporting the INF decision, the implication of his initiative was that Washington was not negotiating seriously enough, even if Trudeau also believed this true of Moscow as well.

In Canada, the general interpretation of Trudeau's move was that Ottawa was finally speaking out on its own, no longer restraining itself in deference to Washington. That Canada had continued to support the cruise and Pershing deployment that was responsible for the breakdown of the negotiations was hardly considered. Nothing came of the Trudeau initiatives, however, and the arms control talks began again a year later in the spring of 1985. But already by February 1984, Trudeau had announced his intention to resign. By June 1984 he was gone, replaced as prime minister by the new Liberal leader, John Turner, who in turn lost his parliamentary majority and his job to Brian Mulroney and the Progressive Conservatives in September 1984. The "peace initiative" had been Trudeau's last hurrah. Having earlier destroyed Canada's military credibility, he nearly tarnished Canada's reputation among its allies irreparably.

Fortunately, the Mulroney government has adopted a more realistic approach to arms control. The Tories have emphasized that what influence Canada does possess in fostering arms control can best be patiently exercised without fanfare through contacts with like-minded states at multilateral forums and in constant consultation with allies, especially the United States during the course of the U.S.-Soviet arms control negotiations in Geneva. The Reagan administration has welcomed this new approach on the part of the Canadian government. Thus, the Quebec declaration on security included promises of consultation on arms control matters, and the president invited the prime minister to contact him at any time concerning the Geneva talks.

Canadian Arms and Canadian Influence

The Mulroney government has also declared that Canada's voice will be listened to more intently on arms control matters if Canada begins to strengthen its contributions to conventional deterrence. Indeed, given the public mood in Canada, one of the strongest arguments the Tories believe they can make for increased defense expenditures is that such spending will further Canada's role as a seeker of disarmament. As put somewhat more directly by Richard Gwyn, respected Ottawa editor of the *Toronto Star*, "The presumption is that the Yanks will only listen to us once we've put our defence money where our peacemaking mouth is."[13]

This approach to Canada's alliance commitments is very much in the tradition of past governments. It is the belief that Canadian arms buy Canadian influence in world councils. It dates back to Canada's participation in World War I. During that struggle, Canada watched with horror as British generals expended tens of thousands of Canadian lives without bringing victory one step closer. Disenchantment grew in Canada and in the other dominions. They demanded a voice in the higher direction of the common effort and successfully pressed for the establishment of an Imperial War Cabinet in 1917. Here David Lloyd George presided as the prime ministers of the dominions sought to influence British policy. For the Canadian prime minister, Robert L. Borden, it also served as a forum in which he could "express the vitality of a young nation through participation in the affairs, responsibilities and dangers of a greater empire."[14]

This was Canada's first real "seat at the table," the opportunity to sit in on and participate in deliberations on matters of global importance that directly affected Canada, but from which Canada, as a less than great power, might well be excluded. The Imperial War Cabinet led to a seat at the Versailles Peace Conference and then recognition as a fully independent country through membership separate from Britain in the League of Nations. All this was believed to have been bought by the undeniably major sacrifices Canada had made during the war.

Toward the end of World War II and in the immediate postwar years, Canada pinned great hopes on the United Nations. Here again the belief was that the country's outstanding war effort would translate into influence within the new world body. When it became clear to Canada that the UN would not serve as an instrument of real collective security, Ottawa worked for the creation of NATO. And when, after the outbreak of the Korean War, the alliance concluded that it needed standing forces to maintain the peace, Canada all but rebuilt its army, navy, and air force to meet NATO's needs. Most important, it sent nearly 10 thousand troops and 12 air squadrons to Europe.

Canada did so because it sincerely believed that such forces were necessary and that contributions from Canada could make a difference. But Ottawa also believed that unless it made such contributions it would not have an adequate say in the direction of the common effort. Arms bought influence – influence with the European governments and influence in Washington. Over the years, this belief was to become the single most salient factor in explaining the posture of the Canadian Armed Forces. Even when both the absolute and relative size of Canada's contributions had become so low that no one, not even Canadian officials, claimed they were militarily significant, the political significance of those contributions was still considered unassailable.

So powerful has this belief been that it played a major role in the formulation of defense policy during the Trudeau era. Trudeau came into office determined to cut back Canada's defense expenditures significantly and reorient the remaining forces to more "national" tasks such as protection of Canada's sovereignty. At first, this meant a total withdrawal of all forces stationed in Europe, although not a Canadian withdrawal from the alliance itself. The prime minister was persuaded to leave a token presence in Germany to preserve Canadian influence in allied councils, which explains the current state of CFE. That force is meant to be only a politically symbolic commitment. For Canada, a physical presence in Germany demonstrates Canada's solidarity with its allies, especially the Germans, and the necessary price – the minimum price – to secure influence in allied councils. To a lesser, yet still relevant extent, this applied to Canada's Norwegian and maritime commitments as well. They have been maintained despite the growing gap between capabilities and commitments because Ottawa has believed that any tampering with the scope of its allied obligations would undermine whatever influence Canada might exercise.

It is of course difficult to determine exactly what kind of influence Canada has had or even seeks to have on the alliance. It is hard to argue that things would have gone differently during the past 40 years if Canada had not had its seat at the table. Overall, Ottawa has supported every major allied decision from reliance upon nuclear weapons, to flexible response, to the INF compromise.

This is not to suggest that Canada has had nothing to contribute to allied deliberations, but rather that its role has been a decidedly modest one. As former Canadian Ambassador to NATO John Halstead has observed, "Canada does not seek a mediating role between allies, but a 'bridging' one, an interpreter seeking to further mutual understanding and to maximize common ground." This role is entirely in Canada's interest for, as Halstead adds, "any lessening of transoceanic ties would be to Canada's disadvantage."[15]

This bridging or consensus-building role is not the same as a policy-initiating role. Canada has not taken, and remains unlikely to take, the lead in proposing major departures from existing NATO political or military doctrines. Those in Canada calling for a more independent foreign policy cite this lack of initiative as proof that alliance membership constrains Ottawa from following policies better suited to Canadian interests or to the Canadian view of the world. All is subordinated to the need for allied unity.

But what would Canada have its allies do or change?

What would a distinctive Canadian approach to NATO strategy look like? Is it really in Canada's interests for there to be expressions of allied diversity?

At present, Canada supports the overall strategic doctrine of the alliance: reliance on the U.S. nuclear deterrent, both strategic and theater, while adding flexibility to the NATO posture through conventional force building. This represents the minimal level of common agreement that has thus far bound the allies together and maintained the peace.

How would Canada change this? Would it, for example, take up the cause of "no first use"? There may be something to be said for this view. Yet the stronger argument is to be made for the maintenance of a nuclear-first-use option in the face of the continued superiority of Soviet conventional forces. To get its allies to renounce this option Canada would have to convince the Europeans and the Americans to augment their conventional forces substantially. Even if Canada were to show its seriousness about no first use by vastly expanding its own conventional forces, a highly unlikely possibility, there is no reason to believe that either the Europeans or Americans would follow suit. More important, an intra-alliance debate over first use would be inconclusive at best—because it would center around untested assumptions—and be highly divisive at worst—because it would spotlight areas of strategic disagreement that most allies wish to avoid. Not even the renowned skill of Canada's diplomats could mold a new strategic consensus under these circumstances.

Canada owes whatever influence it has within NATO to the skill of its diplomats rather than to its military contributions to collective defense. There is no reason to believe that specific levels of Canadian expenditures or specific kinds of commitments make a difference in terms of Canada's bridging role within allied councils. This, of course, is directly contrary to the accepted wisdom in Ottawa. Nonetheless, nowhere outside Canadian governmental and academic circles does anyone link Canadian influence within NATO, which for that matter is hardly ever mentioned outside Canada, to

Canada's defense posture. And no better proof of this can be found than in reviewing the history of the 1970s. Despite the severe cuts by Trudeau, Canada continued to participate actively in allied councils, including the Nuclear Planning Group. The 1970s were active years for Canada in NATO. Canada joined in deliberations on arms control, human rights, and a host of intra-alliance issues. Trudeau had been right all along; Canada could have its seat at the table and as much participation as it wished for half the price.

Some have argued, however, that the Trudeau cuts did undermine Canada's overall relations with Europe, in particular the prospects for strengthening economic links between Canada and the European Community. The strengthening of those links was a central feature of Canada's so-called Third Option, adopted by the Trudeau government in 1972. Under this strategy, Canada was to reduce its economic vulnerability vis-à-vis the United States by increasing the percentage of its trade with other regions of the world, mainly Europe. When Canada approached Germany with the request for a contractual link with the European Community, Chancellor Helmut Schmidt allegedly told Prime Minister Trudeau bluntly, "No tanks, no trade," a reference to Canada's reluctance to outfit its forces in Germany with German tanks and, more generally, to make the point that Canada could not expect to obtain special standing with the Community while reducing its commitments to NATO.

Ironically, in 1949 Canada insisted that the North Atlantic Treaty make reference to the importance of economic cooperation among the allies. Article II of the treaty became known as the "Canadian" article. By its terms, the allies pledged themselves to "eliminate conflict in their international economic policies and . . . encourage economic collaboration." Always viewed with skepticism and at times frustration by Canada's military allies, the notion that military cooperation somehow required economic cooperation and that Canada's military contributions to NATO should afford it special consideration in European economic policies became dogma in the Canadian foreign policy establishment.

But, in reality, the Europeans had never accepted the notion and had conducted their economic relations with Canada irrespective of Canada's NATO contributions. Canada did buy Leopard tanks from Germany, but it seems that the Germans were reviving the ghost of Article II only to sell their weapons and, if possible, to prevent further decreases in Canada's standing contributions. Nothing since that time validates the assertion that Canada's limited rearmament of the mid-1970s has secured stronger economic ties with the European Community. Indeed, the percentage of trade with the United States increased in the 1970s and 1980s.

In their relations with the United States, the European allies have indicated a decided preference for decoupling economic matters from security considerations. To be sure, there are limits as to how far this decoupling can go, particularly with regard to trade with the Soviet bloc. But as became apparent from the Siberian pipeline dispute and compromise, there is a wide area of European-U.S. economic divergence that is not lessened by the continuing U.S. guarantee of European security. Under these circumstances, Canada cannot expect to be considered any differently.

In sum, despite long held and long cherished beliefs in Ottawa, the size and composition of Canada's contributions to NATO translate into neither significant influence nor measurable economic advantage.

North American Defense: Strategy and Politics

The desire for influence and economic advantage through NATO membership partially explains why Canadian political leaders have been less enthusiastic about bilateral cooperation with the United States in the defense of North America. At first glance this seems strange, for the North American efforts are more directly linked to the physical security of Canada itself. They are also more closely tied to the U.S. nuclear deterrent posture, which is the ultimate guarantor of Canadian security. To the extent that Canada has over the years participated in NORAD, it has enhanced the credibility of the U.S. deterrent by helping to ensure advance warning against a Soviet first strike.

From the Canadian viewpoint the problem with NORAD has not been strategic, but political: Canadian air defense forces are controlled, via a bilateral command, by a U.S. Air Force general. NORAD operates outside the NATO framework, although Canadian government statements have sometimes in the past implied the contrary. True, there is a Canada-United States Regional Planning Group (CUSRPG), which is a NATO organization. But matters relating to bilateral security relations are dealt with through direct Washington-Ottawa discussions, through the Canadian-U.S. Permanent Joint Board on Defense, the Canada-United States Military Cooperation Committee, and, above all, through NORAD. Other NATO members are not directly involved in discussions of North American security. This remains a U.S. preference. The United States has not wanted the Europeans involved in nor has it wanted them even to have special access to the operations and intelligence associated with NORAD. There is no indication that the Europeans, for that matter, have ever been interested in participating in NORAD. Canada has thus been alone in dealing with the United States in North America, without the benefit of other allies upon whom it might rely to influence or oppose U.S. actions. The result has been considerable uneasiness in Canada.

This uneasiness has persisted over the years. A recent essay on Canada's security options argues that although Canada should continue to contribute to both NATO and NORAD, NATO structures "should reflect the fact that NATO defends North America as well as Europe. NORAD should be brought into the NATO framework." It even suggests that some thought be given to having units from European air forces stationed in Canada where they could contribute to bomber defense and reinforce the political ties between the two continents.[16]

Although Canadian concerns have been in keeping with

Canada's long-standing desire to cut an independent figure internationally and to be able to influence U.S. policies, the ambivalence about continental air defense compared to the relatively wide acceptance of the NATO role is difficult to justify. In the Permanent Joint Board, the Military Cooperation Committee, and NORAD, Canada has had a unique opportunity to discuss defense issues one-on-one with the United States, issues that pertained directly to Canada. The presence of other allies would only complicate the situation and get in the way of the close and effective Canadian-U.S. military ties.

More fundamentally, it would have been inconsistent at best for Canada to have been an active and contributing member of NATO, yet to have rejected a structured arrangement for North American defense. It would have been hard for Canada to have supported the need for the European allies to accept an extensive U.S. presence on their soil and a highly integrated and elaborate command arrangement while refusing a much smaller U.S. presence in Canada and far less elaborate command arrangements. Ironically, had NORAD been fully integrated into NATO, the United States, with the support of other allies, might have justifiably asked Canada to accept a greater U.S. presence and more integrated command arrangements covering more than just air forces. Such is the case with SACEUR and the subordinate regional commands. One can scarcely imagine the depth of Canadian reaction to the notion of a Supreme Allied Commander, North America – a U.S. general having control over most of Canada's armed forces.

From the standpoint of collective deterrence, the formal separation between NATO and NORAD is not, however, significant. The Europeans rely on the credibility of the U.S. strategic nuclear deterrent. Measures taken to provide warning of and some protection against a Soviet first strike enhance that credibility. There is, of course, the continuing European dilemma about not wanting the United States to feel itself either too secure or too vulnerable, raising questions about whether the United States would risk New York for London or Bonn. But this dilemma would exist even if NORAD were another NATO command and Europeans participated directly in the defense of the United States and Canada. Apart from the well-known U.S. reluctance to share its most sensitive information with the allies beyond Canada, there is also the practical question of whether the Europeans should be diverting resources away from the European theater to make what could only be a symbolic contribution to NORAD. Only Canada might really welcome a closer formal tie between NORAD and NATO — and this only for politically symbolic reasons.

Although Canadians may have always felt uncomfortable with the Canadian-U.S. air defense relationship, the arrangement did allow Canada to participate actively in the defense of North America, and it provided some measure of surveillance for Canadian airspace. Within NORAD, Canada obtained not so much a seat at the table as a seat at the console. Having largely agreed with the United States that the continent must be defended, Canada could have either attempted to do it alone, a costly alternative, or allowed the United States to do it all, a certain blow to national sovereignty and independence.

After the waning of the bomber threat in the early 1960s, the enduring political uneasiness over NORAD, which dates back to its founding in 1957, was made somewhat more bearable because continental defense in general was not a top U.S. priority. In the late 1960s and 1970s no great strategic debates touched the Canadian-U.S. defense relationship in North America, in sharp contrast to the never-ending controversies that beset U.S. involvement in European defense. Continental air defense and other forms of Canadian-U.S. cooperation involved Canada more closely with nuclear weapons and strategies, but this was largely invisible to the public. Most Canadians knew that Canada maintained conventional land and air forces in Germany, but few were aware that Canadian officers sat alongside U.S. officers at the NORAD headquarters where the first decision in a nuclear war, that of initial attack assessment, would take place. Canadians watched from the sidelines as the European governments grappled with the deployment of U.S. nuclear weapons on their soil. Yet the existence of plans for the dispersal of U.S. aircraft to Canadian bases in the event of a crisis remained largely known only to government officials and academics.

In recent years, with the renewed U.S. emphasis on strategic defense, including the SDI, NORAD has been brought center stage in Canada. No doubt this accounts for much of the uneasiness the Progressive Conservatives appear to have about defense issues in general. No doubt, as well, this accounts for the revival of the old arguments about the lack of influence on U.S. decisions afforded by NORAD participation and the need to link NORAD to NATO. Another variant of this argument would have Canada withdraw from NORAD, yet strengthen its conventional force posture in NATO. This, it is argued, would allow Ottawa to exercise more influence within NATO, and, in cooperation with the Europeans, seek to oppose what is called dangerous U.S. nuclear revisionism. Thus, even for critics of Canadian defense policy, the relationship between arms and influence appears to go largely unquestioned.

National Self-Perceptions

It is all but certain that Canada will remain in NATO and continue to cooperate with the United States in North American air defense. Ottawa will continue to share with its allies those perceptions of the external threat that have bound Canada to collective security for nearly 40 years.

The continuation of allied relationships would also be consistent with the way in which Canadians have perceived themselves and their place in the world for all these years. Canada has long viewed itself as a country that should be involved in the larger political-strategic environment. This too is a manifestation of its historical experience. It is true that throughout its existence as a nation Canada has been allied with world powers and therefore has had an immediate and humbling point of comparison. At the same time, this involvement has fostered the self-perception that Canada is not just an underpopulated, weak nation located next to the United States. During the splendor of the British Empire, Canadians could with perfect right regard themselves as part of a global institution. This went beyond Canada's constitutional and juridical ties to London. The empire gave Canada a place in the world that it would not have had if England had abandoned it completely. The description of Canada as a "senior dominion" within the empire reflected the desire on the part of Canadians to identify with issues and events that did not directly touch on Canadian interests.

The experience of the two world wars reinforced these self-perceptions. Canadians entered the postwar era with unprecedented confidence backed up by a tremendous expansion of economic strength. Canada's diplomats were determined to play a role in the shaping of peace and the establishment of a more stable and just world order.

As Canada stepped out on to the world stage in 1945, it stepped into the shadow of the United States, no longer just a great and powerful neighbor, but an atomic superpower in an international system that, despite the best hopes of Canadians (and Americans), soon became increasingly bipolar and dangerous. Ironically, though, the Cold War years were to be the halcyon days of Canadian diplomacy. Canadians believed it was important to participate in the global affairs of the new era in spite of the fact that these were also the days of the Pax Americana. A Pax Americana was not what Canada had had in mind for the postwar world, but, because Ottawa shared Washington's view of the danger of the Soviet Union, Canada understood that "for the time being the United States alone could provide the sinews for the pax and therefore must remain strong." Thus during this period, "Canadian actors saw themselves as loyal and responsible allies and associates in a good cause."[17]

Above all, close cooperation with the United States in security matters went hand in hand with the importance Canada had assumed in matters of international economics and finance. At the World Bank, the International Monetary Fund, and within the efforts toward the establishment of a General Agreement on Tariffs and Trade (GATT), Canada was indeed a major participant. In later years, Canada would be accepted as a full member of the elite group of seven industrial democracies.

In the economic sphere, Canada's claim to major nation status was backed up by the strength of its economy relative to the rest of the world. On security matters, however, Canada rather quickly slipped behind other members of the NATO alliance and certainly could not claim any position of military significance outside the North Atlantic region. Yet membership in NATO and even in NORAD was always viewed as consistent with Canada's high economic standing, despite shifts in the relative standings of the allies.

Today, continued involvement in Western security allows Canadians to see their country as somehow having an impact on the great strategic decisions of the day or at least being privy to what others have decided. These decisions may not all directly affect Canada. But without its alliance memberships Canada would play almost no role whatsoever in these global deliberations, undermining Canada's nationhood.

Because Canada's political leaders have understood how important it is for Canada to play a global role, Canada's military personnel have been afforded the opportunity to participate in what can be described as world-class operations. This has been especially the case since 1945. Without Canadian-U.S. defense cooperation and NATO, not only would Canada's military leaders have had a hard time justifying expenditures in the nuclear age, they would have been excluded from joining with the larger and more sophisticated forces of the allies. Apart from any consideration of specific Canadian national interests, it is in the professional interest of the armed forces to be involved in the land and air defense of central Europe, the maritime defense of the Atlantic, and the air and maritime defense of North America. Historically, Canada's forces have always fought alongside and against those of the great powers. This has been integral to Canada's military heritage. The postwar alliances allowed the military to continue this tradition. NATO and cooperation in North American defense gave the Royal Canadian Navy, the Canadian Army, and the Royal Canadian Air Force their raison d'être in the nuclear age.

The alliance relationships also helped the forces sustain the trauma of unification, for the one thing unification has not changed is the structure of Canada's alliance commitments. Membership has been retained in NATO and NORAD — and therefore the world-class roles for the forces. No specific commitment within the alliance was eliminated and indeed, a new, and in many ways more daring one, that of the reinforcement of Norway's defenses, was added. To be sure, the forces have suffered grievously as a result of the decline in defense expenditures and the deterioration of their equipment. They have also, no doubt, felt their honor threatened as it became increasingly clear that Canada could not live up to its obligations. And they have felt pangs of embarrassment as they attended allied meetings and took up individual positions on allied staffs. But attend they did, and they would not have been able to do so if Canada had not maintained its alliance roles.

In part, the desire of the armed forces to remain involved in the military postures of Canada's allies explains the persistent fragmentation of the country's defense posture today. The air force has, at least in the past, wanted to have a role in Germany as well as one in North American air defense. For the ground forces, withdrawal from the central front would mean the abandonment of the heavy armor role. Mobile Command would no longer be able to participate with the Americans and Germans in major land exercises. And Canada's sailors, if excluded from NATO and North American roles, would find themselves quickly relegated to the status of a coast guard or fishing patrol.

The armed forces are, to be sure, encouraged to maintain all these roles by allied military leaders. What U.S. or NATO commander would turn away any allied contribution regardless of size? Moreover, Canada's navy, air force, and army personnel are among the West's best. They are well trained, highly professional, and disciplined. There is no doubt that, if adequately reequipped, the Canadian Armed Forces would be able to make an outstanding contribution in all of their present allied roles. Unfortunately, they are not so well endowed and have not been for at least a decade. The problem is not just the lack of money, it is that they are overcommitted given the amount of money that has been available. In this, Canada's political leadership, in particular past Liberal governments, have received from the Canadian military better service than the leadership deserved.

At the same time, the desire on the part of the armed forces to maintain all elements of Canada's fragmented alliance contributions has only served to reinforce the political leadership's view that all commitments should be preserved to secure Canada's role in the Western alliance. To withdraw from a commitment would deprive some part of the armed forces of a modern role, but, of course, it is the fragmentation of the defense posture that largely accounts for the fact that the military is not equipped to fulfill any of its commitments well.

If Canada's political leaders have never seriously considered restructuring the country's defense posture, neither apparently have its military leaders, at least not in public. And this is the case despite the existence of a unified headquarters, the absence of competing service chiefs, and the presence of a single chief of the defence staff. In fact, Canadians consider themselves not only eligible for participation in the joint conventional deterrence posture of the West, but are reluctant to be excluded from any part of that common endeavor, regardless of how little Canada's contribution is to any part of it.

3

Emphasizing the Assets: The Choice in Defense Policy

The Need to Choose

On the eve of a new white paper on defense, Canada faces a choice. In 1986, its defense efforts rest on what Nicholas Stethem of the Toronto-based Strategic-Analysis Group has called a "cosmetic ability," a "let's-pretend capability."[18] Either it can continue to pretend and try to prop up the several fragmented and marginal contributions it makes to collective security or it can restructure its defense effort, dropping some roles to strengthen fundamentally the remaining, and more important, ones. As he prepares his white paper, Minister of National Defence Erik Nielsen will have to face the fact that the money is not there to enhance all of the country's NATO roles to make them more than token contributions and to repair shortcomings in the NORAD contributions as well. Indeed, his department may not even have sufficient capital resources over the next 10 to 15 years to continue the propping up operations it has been engaged in. By default, if not by ministerial decision, one or several roles will further decay, if not be totally abandoned. Too many aging weapon systems will need replacing, and manpower will still be stretched too thinly.

The capital budget of the Department of National

Defence for 1984–1985 was approximately C$2.5 billion (U.S. $1.85 billion). This small sum will rise gently in coming years. But even if it were substantially increased as part of a 6 percent hike in overall defense spending, it would still be insufficient to meet the current sea, land, and air needs.

In the summer of 1985 MARCOM celebrated the seventy-fifth anniversary of the Royal Canadian Navy. It was a curious celebration. Not only has the Royal Canadian Navy ceased to exist since the unification of the forces in the late 1960s, but it was clear that there was very little to rejoice about, given the present state of Canada's maritime forces under whatever nomenclature or command structure. As modern warships from a dozen allied nations crowded into Halifax harbor as part of the celebrations, Canadians could see for themselves how unfavorably their fleet compared with that of even relatively small maritime powers such as Norway, Italy, and the Federal Republic of Germany. It was a far cry from the brave days of World War II when the navy supplied nearly half the ships in the crucial Battle of the Atlantic, or even from the Cold War era when a rearmed Canadian navy provided nearly 40 major combatants to Western collective security. Thus, intermingled with nostalgia for these bygone days, were critical comments about the state of MARCOM today. One newspaper even suggested that the heavy expenditures for the celebration had resulted in less money being available for fuel and supplies; consequently, the amount of time Canada's ships could spend at sea had been cut back. As if to revive the spirit of older days and boost morale, the celebrations were used to showcase MARCOM's "new" uniforms—the old navy blue of the Royal Canadian Navy, restored by order of the minister of national defence.

But it will take more than new attire to give Canada's sailors the first-class force the prime minister called for. Canada is a three-ocean country, yet MARCOM is barely able to provide adequate forces for one ocean. It has long been committed to support the NATO posture at sea, but even the Department of National Defence admits that it is failing to meet this obligation. In its NATO roles, its North American roles, and even in its responsibilities for the protection of sovereignty, MARCOM is currently confronting a commitment-capability gap that will only grow larger in the coming years. So bleak does MARCOM's future appear at the moment that senior defense officials are warning about having only a 10-ship fleet by the mid-1990s. Not only will MARCOM have even less to celebrate at the time of its eighty-fifth anniversary, it may well have insufficient forces to celebrate with.

It is true that in the case of maritime forces, numbers tell only half the story. Quality, geographic, and political considerations must all be included in any assessment of a country's seapower. Yet numbers are important especially when they become so small that other factors cannot compensate for the inherent loss of credibility. Table 1 shows the composition of Canada's maritime forces immediately before unification and the severe cuts of the early 1970s. It compares them first with the current situation, second with the situation in 1996 if existing procurement plans are implemented, and finally with the recommendations of a Canadian Senate committee report released in 1983.

Behind the numbers is an even more telling story. Only 4 of Canada's 20 surface combatants are less than 15 years old. These are the Tribal class destroyers built in the 1970s, the last such ships built. The remaining 16 are of 1950s or early 1960s vintage. Plans for a new Canadian Patrol Frigate (CPF) have been discussed since the early 1970s. In 1977, the Liberal government approved a target force level of 24 fully capable surface ships. It was not until 1983, however, that final approval was given for the construction of the first batch of six CPFs and not until 1985 that the keel was laid for the initial vessel, with delivery not expected until 1989. Costs for the six frigates are estimated at C$4.5 billion. Subsequent batches—necessary if MARCOM is not to become a 10-ship fleet—can be expected to cost at least the same.

But ships are not enough. The CPFs will be equipped

TABLE 1
Canada's Maritime Forces 1966–1996

Type	1966	Current Levels	1996 Under Present Plans	Senate Committee 1996 Recommendations
Aircraft Carriers	1	0	0	0
Destroyers/Frigates	33	20	10*	16**
Submarines	4 (by 1969)	3	3	20
Operational Support Ships	2	3	3	3
Diving Support Ships	1	1	1	1
Minehunters	0	0	0	4
Minesweepers	6	0	0	9
Fast Patrol Boats	0	0	0	12
Long-Range Patrol Aircraft	36	18	18	36
Coastal Patrol Aircraft	18	18	18	18
ASW Helicopters	18	35	35	45
Attack Aircraft	0	0	0	84***
Merchant Ships	0	0	0	3

*If decision is not made to build six more Canadian Patrol Frigates (CPF).

**This assumes a follow-on six CPF plus reliance on four refitted Tribal class destroyers.

***Air-to-Surface equipped F-18s drawn from Air Command.

Sources: International Institute for Strategic Studies (IISS), *The Military Balance, 1966–1967* (London: IISS, 1966); Canada, Senate, Standing Committee on Foreign Affairs, Subcommittee on National Defence, Report, *Canada's Maritime Defence* (Ottawa: Minister of Supply and Services, 1983).

with the most modern naval weaponry available. This will include such U.S. systems as the RIM-7 Seasparrow surface-to-air missile, the Harpoon surface-to-surface missile, the Phalanx antimissile defense system, and the SURTASS towed array sensor. Each CPF will carry a single antisubmarine warfare (ASW) helicopter and also deploy advanced torpedoes. But only six frigates have been approved for construction. The Tribals are also to be refitted with more modern equipment under the Tribal Update and Modernization Project (TRUMP), which will prolong their usefulness until the end of the century. Older ships are being patched up to await the deployment of the CPFs in the 1990s.

Canada's three obsolete Oberon class submarines were acquired from the British in the early 1960s. Their use at this time is mainly to provide mock targets for ASW exercises. The Defence Department has begun to look into the acquisition of modern electric-powered submarines and will consider bids from foreign builders for batches of 4, 8, or 12. Estimates for even the lowest batch of four are set around C$1 billion. Other Defence Department studies are directed at the possibility of acquiring small combat craft to serve in a patrol and even minesweeping role. No such vessels are currently in the inventory.

The situation for naval aviation is only somewhat better. As part of the Trudeau cutbacks, Canada sold its only ASW aircraft carrier for scrap and deployed the carrier's surveillance planes and helicopters to land bases. But in the mid-1970s, MARCOM acquired a new LRPA, dubbed the Aurora, a version of the U.S. Navy's P-3 Orion. Thirty-six of the older LRPAs were replaced by only 18 Auroras, however, and although the Aurora is certainly a capable ASW platform, its small numbers greatly reduce the effectiveness of Canada's long-range naval aviation. Furthermore, the LRPA force must be divided among three oceans. MARCOM's aging Sea King helicopters, which are both land-based and carried by destroyers and frigates and are essential for ASW operations, will also have to be replaced. Replacement could cost on the order of C$2 billion.

The impending rapid decline in MARCOM's inventory of major weapon systems is matched by ammunition shortages. Canada is currently improving its stockpiles with new torpedoes and surface-to-surface weaponry, but more will be required in the coming years even if the size of the surface and maritime air forces remains constant.

In short, the rebuilding of MARCOM, even if it were to include only major weapon systems such as more patrol frigates, submarines, and LRPAs, is going to be extremely expensive. It would be quite easy to spend the bulk of defense capital funds simply on rescuing MARCOM as a viable naval operation. Indeed, maritime capital expenditures alone could be equal to a sum nearly double the currently projected increases in Canada's entire defense spending.

But CFE will also generate heavy new capital needs, beyond the CF-18s that are currently being acquired and beyond the low-level air defense system, for which a contractor will be named shortly. The tactical environment on Europe's central front is in the midst of technological change as the Soviets improve their armor and night-fighting capabilities and as NATO, largely in response, considers the implementation of new tactics such as "assault breaker" and "deep strike." The 4CMBG already requires new short-range rockets to replace its aging Carl Gustavs, which cannot be effectively used against new improved armor. New medium and long-range weapons will also be required. Similarly, new and extremely costly antiarmor munitions will be needed, along with armored artillery ammunition vehicles. The 4CMBG operates with only scout helicopters (similar to those relied upon by radio stations in North America to give traffic reports), which themselves will shortly require an upgrading, whereas U.S. Army and other NATO armies rely on attack helicopters as essential in antitank operations. To remain effective, the 4CMBG may have to be equipped with these.

Extremely sophisticated new communications technology will also be required if the 4CMBG is to remain fully integrated in NATO's command and control system. A chemical warfare decontamination unit, a range of night-fighting equipment, and a variety of light vehicles is also needed. In short, as Professor David Cox of Queen's University in Kingston, Ontario has convincingly demonstrated, for Canada "to maintain an armoured role in the future European battlefield will be extraordinarily expensive—it is not too far-fetched to argue that capital expenditures in the order of $10 billion will be required over the next decade."[19] But that will not be the end. Over the next decade the Defence Department will have to begin considering how to replace or upgrade significantly the Leopard tanks with which the 4CMBG and FMC units in Canada are equipped.

Even if reequipped, the 4CMBG would remain undermanned. Its full peacetime establishment has consisted of 3,200 personnel, which was only about 60 percent of its wartime establishment, far below the NATO criteria of some 90 percent. Troops numbering 2,400 would have had to be airlifted from FMC units in Canada to bring the 4CMBG up to strength. If physically possible, others would later be brought in to provide additional strength and replace casualties. The minister of national defence announced in 1985 that CFE would be strengthened by 1,200, most of whom will go to the 4CMBG. But three problems remain. First, the 4CMBG will still not be at wartime levels. Second, augmentation efforts will be difficult to undertake. The departure of troops for Germany and for the northern flank as part of the CAST and AMF(L) commitments would all but denude the FMC of regular troops in Canada, especially given the poor state of the reserves. Canada, as well, has never carried out a full test of the augmentation exercise, which would have to be undertaken in uncertain crisis conditions at rapid speed. The Senate committee found that "augmentation seems an uncertain prospect at this time. It might prove completely impractical in various circumstances." Finally, even if augmentation were successfully completed, the 4CMBG would be too small a force to undertake the tasks assigned to it, which would require, according to various expert witnesses who testified before the committee, a standing brigade group of about 7,600 troops in peacetime.

CFE's other combat unit, 1CAG, is being equipped with CF-18s to replace its aging CF-104s, officially called "Starfighters," unofficially, "Widowmakers." One of CFE's most glaring weaknesses, the absence of low-level air defenses at the Lahr and Baden airfields, will soon be remedied. Its ammunition stocks are probably insufficient, however, leading to the prospect that early on in a conflict it would exhaust its armaments. Moreover, the 1CAG still lacks the capability to carry out airfield runway, tarmac, and dispersal repairs or to dispose of unexploded bombs. The 1CAG also has been manned at only about 60 percent of its wartime level, a deficiency that will only partially be overcome through CFE's new manning levels. Bringing it to war strength will also require augmentation from Canada.

Several improvements are under way that will affect Canada's northern flank commitments. The acquisition by AIRCOM of CF-18s will lead to the retirement of the old CF-5s with which it would have to exercise its commitment to send, in the event of an emergency, two squadrons of aircraft to northern Norway. Elements of the low-level air defense system would be deployed with the CAST Brigade Group, which itself will be test deployed for the first time in 1986. The troubling "double tasking" of the same Canadian battalion to both the AMF(L) and the CAST Brigade Group has been ended, strengthening both.

Yet nagging worries persist about both the air and land commitments to the NATO northern flank. AIRCOM officials are concerned that they will have too few CF-18s in Canada to meet both NORAD and NATO northern flank commitments. Under normal circumstances, the total number of nontraining aircraft in Canada's four tactical fighter squadrons will be only 32, although presumably some aircraft used for training could be impressed for emergency uses. Although some Canadian military equipment for the CAST Brigade Group is being pre-positioned in northern Norway, most would have to be transported across the North Atlantic and Norwegian Sea in Norwegian merchant vessels specially impressed for that task. Although there is reputed to be an excellent computerized system for requisitioning vessels, transit time would be roughly a month. It is therefore hard to conceive of any military utility for the CAST Brigade Group as presently constituted. To get the Brigade Group to Norway before hostilities commenced, NATO would need 30 days advance warning, which is itself most unlikely. If the CAST Brigade Group were dispatched after the commencement of hostilities, it is difficult to believe that both personnel and equipment would be able both to cross the sea and disembark in Norway.

The area to which the Brigade Group is assigned, northern Norway, is adjacent to the Kola Peninsula, the home port of the Soviet Northern Fleet, where Soviet forces are concentrated extremely heavily. In the early days of any conflict, NATO and the Soviets would most probably fight a fierce naval struggle in the Norwegian Sea. At the very least, NATO would attempt to seal off the Greenland-Iceland-United Kingdom (GIUK) gap. The Brigade Group would be especially useful in aiding in this struggle, but it also makes it doubtful that the group's merchant shipping could make it to the designated ports in Norway after the opening of the sea battle. Not surprisingly, the Senate committee called for a review of the CAST commitment. To make it viable would require not only a more extensive pre-positioning of equipment, but greater airlift capability. The Defence Department is only beginning to come to grips with the need to replace the five Boeing 707s and 27 slow-moving Hercules heavy transport aircraft of AIRCOM's Air Transport Group toward the end of the decade. The Senate committee has also conducted hearings on that subject.

As a result of the decline in the bomber threat to North America, NORAD's air defenses were downgraded over the past two and a half decades. Recently, both the U.S. and Canadian governments have recognized that elements of the aging system need to be replaced, if only to retain its detection capabilities and to improve them to deal with the emerging threat posed by cruise missiles and a new generation of Soviet bombers. Canada's participation in North American air defense is accordingly being enhanced. But there are still some major gaps. AIRCOM's aging CF-101 Voodoos, of 1950s vintage, will be replaced by CF-18s. To repeat, however, there is substantial concern that the 138 aircraft will not be enough to cover North American, German, and northern flank commitments as well as losses due to attrition. Under the original contract with McDonnell Douglas, the government had an option to purchase an additional 20 aircraft at the original price. That option was allowed to lapse, though, by the Mulroney government in April 1985.

Under the terms of agreements signed at the Shamrock summit in March 1985, the North American air defense system will be considerably improved by the United States and Canada, especially insofar as radar is concerned, with the United States paying the bulk of the costs. The United States has been proceeding apace with the construction of several Over-the-Horizon Backscatter (OTH-B) radar stations, which will provide coverage fanning several hundred miles outward on the east and west coasts and on the U.S. southern flank. These stations, which are located in and paid for by the United States, will also provide coverage for Canadian Atlantic and Pacific approaches to the continent; data from them will be provided, under NORAD auspices, to AIRCOM's air defense headquarters in North Bay, Ontario. In return, Canada will jointly man the OTH-B sites providing coverage of Canadian airspace. OTH-B radar cannot, however, be pointed northward, as disturbances from the aurora borealis can disrupt it. Hence the DEW line is being replaced by the 13 long-range and 39 short-range stations of the North Warning System, which, like the DEW line before it, will run from east to west in the high Alaskan and Canadian Arctic and then down the Labrador coast, completing the peripheral coverage of the North American continent.

The problem, from the Canadian point of view, is the center, or more precisely the populated regions of southern Canada located to the north of the border with the United States. Radar coverage in this region is currently being provided by the CADIN (Continental Air Defense Integrated

North)-Pinetree line, a chain erected in the early 1950s. It, too, is obsolete, and, in accordance with the North American air defense modernization agreements, will be closed down soon on a Canadian-U.S. shared cost basis. This will leave the region without ground-based military radar coverage. The United States recently constructed on its territory shared military-civilian radar facilities, the Joint Surveillance System (JSS). Canada, though, for the now-familiar reason – a shortage of money – built only new civilian radars for the Department of Transport, the data from which is not shared with AIRCOM. The "hole" could be covered by Airborne Warning and Control System (AWACS) aircraft. But Canada has none. The U.S. Air Force has 34, only 8 of which are designated for possible NORAD use and some are comanned by U.S. Air Force and AIRCOM crews. But their numbers are far too limited to provide anything remotely close to continuous coverage.

The southern parts of Canada will generally also be out of range for overflights by CF-18s. Partially because of the impending absence of radar there and partially because of the decision to make the best military use out of the not so numerous new aircraft, the CF-18s will not only be deployed in the north, at air bases and forward operating locations, but will also be "pointing northward."

The "hole" in the Canadian middle has little consequence for the detection of Soviet bombers and cruise missiles, because these would be picked up in the north by the North Warning System and on the coasts by the OTH-B radars. The problem, from the Canadian point of view, is the loss of the ability to exercise sovereignty over aircraft entering Canada from the south, that is, of course, from the United States. It has been an article of faith in recent years that that exercise is a prime purpose of the Canadian air defense forces, a point of view shared by politicians and many senior military officials alike. Thus, when NORAD acquired new regional operations control centers (ROCCs) several years ago, the air defense boundaries were redrawn so that Canadian officials could direct Canadian aircraft in Canadian airspace.

A new ROCC was built at North Bay to control western Canadian airspace, joining the facility that had long controlled the east. Previously, western Canadian airspace had been controlled by a facility located in the United States. These new arrangements did not mean that U.S. air defense aircraft were barred from entering Canadian airspace. To the contrary, NORAD remains predicated on such cross-border operations. It does mean, though, that short of an attack on North America, Canadian aircraft, under the control of Canadian air defense facilities, should be available to enforce Canadian sovereignty. This would particularly include enforcement of Canadian regulations over noncompliant aircraft, such as straying airliners.

"Sovereignty" itself, as well as its military applications, is hard to define. There has, for example, been little public debate over how great a threat the possibility of straying aircraft constitutes. But the concept has been adhered to tenuously, even emotionally, in Canada. Lurking behind the idea is the worry that Canada could lose control of its airspace to its huge neighbor to the south. The 1971 defense white paper issued by the Trudeau government placed major emphasis on sovereignty protection, calling it the prime mission of the Canadian Armed Forces. It is also written into the current NORAD agreement. Erik Nielsen, in announcing the North Warning agreement, called the system an improvement in Canada's sovereignty protection capability, both in that it will be Canadian operated and will continue to allow Canadian forces to detect aircraft entering Canadian airspace from the north. At any rate, it tends to raise strong emotions. As the commander of AIRCOM testified,

> I instinctively, as I think most Canadians do, have a feeling that unless we have the capability of controlling our airspace — that is, of knowing of the presence of an intruder and being able to intercept and identify that intruder to enforce our sovereignty in airspace — there is something lacking in the composition of the Canadian

nation. It is a difficult question (and one that calls, not for) a military expression of the need but essentially a political one.[20]

Such a political expression may soon occur once the CADIN-Pinetree line is shut down and AIRCOM's Fighter Group shifts its interceptors away from southern Canada to more northerly orientations. Either the government will have to abandon the now widely held notions of the sovereignty role for Canadian air defense forces or it will have to find the interceptors and radar capability to plug the gap. Fighter aircraft are in very short supply. The acquisition of new radar coverage, if it took the form of AWACS aircraft, would have to be purchased, a most expensive proposition. Production lines are being shut down for U.S. AWACS of the kind that will be allocated on a limited basis to NORAD. An alternative would be to equip Aurora-type aircraft with an AWACS package. Still another alternative would be to accept temporarily the deficiencies and wait until (presumably expensive) space-based radars are available, perhaps as early as within a decade.

The issue has all the makings of a major controversy in Canada, once the implications of the new deployments are publicly grasped. "Who cost Canada its sovereignty?" is the question likely to asked in the partisan environment of the Canadian House of Commons. The Progressive Conservatives will point the finger at the Liberals. Despite the emphasis the Liberal government placed on sovereignty while it was in power, it neglected to replace the CADIN-Pinetree line with a JSS-type system that could provide surveillance in southern Canadian airspace or acquire AWACS aircraft. The Liberals will try to pin the blame on the Tories. After all, it was the Mulroney government that signed the modernization agreements, which included shutting the CADIN-Pinetree line down. If such a controversy does break out, it would be unfortunate for Canadian-U.S. air defense cooperation, for it could serve to reinforce the notion, held by many skeptical

Canadians, that participation in NORAD costs Canada its sovereignty. With or without such a controversy, there will be strong pressure within Canada to buy the systems needed to plug the gap.

Opting Out Entirely

One solution to the problem of the fragmentation of the Canadian Armed Forces is to opt out of the defense of Europe, or of North America, or both. After all, it is these commitments that are generating the demands for the kinds and numbers of military forces that Canada is simply no longer able to provide. A withdrawal from NATO would mean that Canada would not have to worry greatly about the cost of new artillery, tanks, transport aircraft, foreign basing, surface ships – and the need to decide among these. An abandonment of military cooperation with the United States in the defense of North America would resolve the problem of a lack of submarines, of sufficient fighter aircraft, and of advanced radar capability. Opting out entirely would mean that Canada would explicitly be taking a cost-free ride in terms of its security.

It is not unimaginable that Canada might withdraw from NATO. After all, the NDP has been calling for such a withdrawal for years. And such a withdrawal would certainly solve the problem of the Canadian Armed Forces being stretched unbearably thinly. The FMC could concentrate on aid to the civil power and the training of peacekeeping forces. MAR-COM could enforce fisheries regulations and other manifestations of Canadian sovereignty, although it could be dissolved and those roles turned over to the Coast Guard. AIRCOM's role in North America would remain pretty much the same, although it would benefit from the repatriation of the CF-18s from Europe, and funds could far more easily be found to plug the radar gaps it is facing in the south. But such a step is exceedingly unlikely and undesirable. Participation in NATO not only serves the defense of Canada, it allows Canada to contribute to the defense of Western Europe. Moreover, Canadian governments have sought to use NATO to pursue within it political and even economic interests. Quite simply, Canada needs NATO, a fact recognized by both the Progressive Conservative and Liberal parties and by the Canadian public. The chances of the NDP coming to power are slim. But if it ever did, it would probably discover – as other Western social democratic parties have – that the world looks far different when you are sitting on the government benches and have the responsibility for the country's foreign and defense policies.

Similarly, it is not unimaginable that Canada could cease its continental air defense operations. But that, too, is highly unlikely. Deterrence rests in part on the ability to detect hostile bombers entering Canadian airspace. It is in Canada's interest to contribute to deterrence simply because Canada cannot escape the effects of a nuclear war involving the United States. In addition, if Canadian air defense efforts were discontinued, the United States would be forced to insist that it be permitted to undertake all surveillance operations in Canada. Canada would lose control over its own airspace, an unacceptable development.

On the other hand, over the next decade Canada might very well want to look long and hard at the possibility of dissolving or fundamentally altering NORAD, and the United States might very well want to encourage such a step. The existence of NORAD involves a trade-off for both countries. Both gain from the military efficiency of having a single commander with operational control over the air defense forces of the entire continent. There are political benefits as well. The NORAD agreement constitutes a reassuring symbol. There are political costs, though – in particular, the enduring uneasiness that many Canadians feel about being linked so tightly in the bilateral military arrangement. This uneasiness will grow if the U.S. Unified Space Command becomes involved in military activities with which Canada may not want to associate itself, namely ASAT, and, ultimately, any new antimissile defenses that may emerge from President Reagan's SDI research program.

From the U.S. point of view, there are two drawbacks to the present command structure. First, it is not in the U.S. interest that Canadians become so worried about the implications of NORAD membership that they consider air defense cooperation too expensive politically. Second, unease is growing in the U.S. military establishment about having a foreign power, even as close an ally as Canada, linked to U.S. space developments.

It will remain essential for the security of both the United States and Canada that Canadian airspace be monitored and that there be close cooperation between the air defense operations of the two countries. But this does not mean that a joint command is essential. Although the term NORAD is often used simply to mean continental defense cooperation, the two are not synonymous. Prior to 1957 there was close cooperation between Canadian air defense forces and those of the U.S. Continental Air Defense Command. Data from radar lines were shared. Fighter interceptors could cross the border. Plans were coordinated. By the late 1950s a joint command became desirable so that the scores of interceptor squadrons (more than 60 U.S., 9 Canadian) located across the continent could be drawn upon by a single commander as part of a continent-wide battle plan.

Today, with Canada and the United States having far fewer fighter aircraft than during the heyday of air defense in the late 1950s, the pre-NORAD command relationships could be reestablished and the joint command dissolved. This could prove all the more feasible if new space-based detection systems are devised. The North Warning radar line has been designated a "transition system." If research projects currently under way bear fruit, it will eventually be possible to detect, and possibly even destroy, bombers and cruise missiles from space. The value of Canadian real estate for continental air defense would decline. So would the necessity for a joint command.

Developments in space could have precisely the opposite effect, however. If new space-based antimissile defenses are ever deployed by the United States, continental air defense efforts would continue to increase in importance, beyond the augmentation and replacement of aging systems currently being made to deal with the bomber and cruise missile threat. It would make little sense to defend against missiles while letting bombers through. If space-based detection and destruction systems directed against bombers do not prove feasible, ground-based air defense efforts, including those undertaken in Canada, will become increasingly important.

The rub, for the moment, is in not being able to know whether space technology will make ground-based defenses more or less important. Accordingly, serious thought needs to be given to a first step, taking the "aerospace" out of the North American Aerospace Defense Command, giving it back its original name, the "North American Air Defense Command," and moving it out of Colorado Springs, away from the new U.S. Unified Space Command and away from the controversial Canadian involvement in space-based antimissile defense. If, after a few years, it becomes evident that SDI research will not pan out or is prevented by a new U.S.-USSR agreement from resulting in new antimissile deployments and hence a new and major emphasis on continental air defense is unnecessary, NORAD could either be left in its new location or simply dissolved and replaced with the kind of Canadian-U.S. air defense arrangements that were in effect before 1957. It bears repeating, though, that regardless of the Canadian-U.S. command arrangements, Canada will have an essential interest in maintaining its own air defense forces to protect its sovereignty and help protect the U.S. strategic nuclear deterrent. It is not NORAD per se that is important.

In short, it is in the Canadian interest to continue to provide forces for both the defense of Europe and for the defense of North America. But the Canadian Armed Forces are stretched so thinly that today they make no substantial contributions to the defense of Europe, and there are some potentially serious shortcomings in the North American effort. Given the serious financial limitations, there is little prospect that significant improvements can be made unless some roles are dropped to strengthen others.

Which Roles to Strengthen, Which to Cut?

The Northern Flank

At first glance, it might be thought that the CAST commitment to the defense of Norway should be the prime candidate for termination. And, indeed, many commentators have suggested such a step. After all, as a result of the required transit time, it is little more than a perfunctory pledge. It has been kept by the Canadian government so that it can claim to be honoring its long-standing promise to send a reinforcement unit to Europe. Nonetheless, if the CAST Brigade Group were provided with a combination of sufficient pre-positioned equipment in Norway and adequate air transportation so that its current reliance on Norwegian shipping could by and large be eliminated, it would then constitute a valuable contribution to the defense of NATO Europe. Indeed, a viable CAST commitment is far more useful, in military terms, than the Canadian Brigade Group stationed in Germany.

Norway shares a border with the Soviet Union. In keeping with long-standing policy, it forbids the stationing of nuclear weapons and foreign forces on its territory, lest it provide the Soviet Union with an excuse to charge it with provocative action. It has made clear, though, that if it feels dangerously threatened, the strictures could be removed. Norway's armed forces (including its army of about 40 thousand troops) would have to be reinforced by Norwegian reservists and other NATO forces entirely brought in from the outside in the event of a real or anticipated Soviet attack. Emergency forces are earmarked for deployment to Norway by Canada, the Netherlands, and the United Kingdom. The bulk of outside reinforcements, however, would have to come from the United States under present plans.

Since 1977, the U.S. Marine Corps has been given the task of providing such forces in numbers ranging from 8,000 to 16,000. The United States has also been pre-positioning military equipment in Norway. After that pre-positioning is complete, the entire U.S. force could be airlifted into Norway in two or three days; a sealift would require at least 12 days. Two difficulties exist, though, with the marine commitment. The first is that the marines could be called upon for deployment elsewhere in the world, and in the event of a worldwide emergency, they might not be available for NATO's northern flank. Because of that worldwide commitment, they have also not been able to concentrate heavily on winter warfare training. As defense analyst Charles T. Kamps pointed out,

> Serious questions have been raised about the ability of a Marine brigade to function effectively in the Arctic. Although the Corps reinstituted mountain training in 1976 and continues to provide cold-weather programs, the emphasis is on survival, with little in-depth operational follow-up. Typically, only one battalion gets any real Arctic training each year, and that is much less in duration than British or Canadian training is. This may be excused by the Marines' missions to be able to respond anywhere in the world, but the lack of a dedicated cold-weather force remains a problem.[21]

The other problem, unhappily, and one that appeared during the Norwegian-U.S. discussions over the pre-positioning of U.S. equipment in Norway, is nationality. Some Norwegians have proved sensitive to the possibility of a U.S. military presence in the northern part of their country, close to the Soviet frontier – a sensitivity exacerbated by doses of anti-Americanism left over from the Vietnam War. U.S. stockpiles are therefore to be placed not in the area of northern Norway that the marines would presumably be expected to defend, but, rather, 600 kilometers to the south. As Erling Bjøl has noted in a recent Adelphi Paper,

> The US Marines had been singled out for particular opprobrium by the Scandinavian anti-war lobby and in

Norway, as in Sweden, the "Vietnam generation" had
come into positions of influence. It was felt that, had it
been Canadian equipment, very few would have mind-
ed the prepositioning. Some Norwegians also worried
that Americans might be tempted, if war broke out, to
utilize nuclear weapons in the empty northern regions
of their country.[22]

These problems do not exist with the CAST Brigade
Group. The only area of deployment that has been earmarked
for the Brigade Group is Norway. Winter warfare is a Canadian specialty. Canadian soldiers "are equipped and trained
to live and fight in the most severe conditions of cold and
snow. Canadian mechanized infantrymen frequently leave
their vehicles to carry out airmobile operations or to move
cross country on skis and snowshoes.[23] And, as Bjøl pointed
out, Norwegians are not as sensitive about the Canadian military because of their nationality and because the Canadians
are not equipped or trained to use nuclear weapons. Thus Canadian equipment is being pre-positioned in the Norwegian
north, although Canada does not at the moment have all that
much equipment to spare for location there.

Moreover the CAST Brigade Group, although not large,
would constitute a significant portion of the NATO forces
committed to the defense of Norway. To be sure, the military
might that the Soviet Union has amassed in the Kola Peninsula, across from the the Norwegian frontier, has been called
the greatest concentration of naval, ground, and air forces
to be found anywhere in the world. But even beyond the
traditional advantages afforded the defense, NATO forces in
Norway would enjoy some others, if those forces can be ready
in time. Above all, the northern Norwegian terrain is rough,
marked with fjords, and has just one good north-south artery.

An important political, even psychological, element is
also at play on the northern flank. Because of its own ban
on the stationing of allied troops, Norway is in danger of feeling isolated from the alliance, a sensitivity the Soviets have
tried to exploit in the past. The ultimate result of a combina-

tion of this isolation and Soviet blandishments could be the "Finlandization" of Norway, or a variant thereof, whereby Norway drifts out of NATO. To the extent that the Norwegians can be assured that reinforcements are in readiness, those feelings of isolation can be minimized. Those assurances could be given more visible and compelling form through closer Canadian-Norwegian military cooperation.

NATO has a vital stake in Norway. It is not just a matter of extending the umbrella of collective defense to a particularly exposed member of the alliance. The control of Norway and its air bases would heavily affect Soviet egress into the North Atlantic during a NATO-Warsaw Pact conflict. Similarly, Norwegian fjords would provide ideal dispersal locations for Soviet surface ships and submarines and provide them with replenishment points 600 to 900 miles closer to the shipping lanes of Europe. Thus, if the Soviets are able to seize Norway, their task of interfering with the sea-lanes between North America and Europe, which would be vital for reinforcement of NATO forces, would be made far easier. NATO has therefore a military interest in the strengthening of the CAST Brigade Group to the point at which it becomes a viable military and political commitment.

There is the argument, sometimes made in Canada, that a militarily viable CAST posture would be politically untenable. The reason given is that if the CAST force is postured to arrive in Norway in advance of hostilities, as it must if it is to be of use, it would mean that the Canadian government would have to make a decision to send this reinforcement during a period of unprecedented East-West tension, in the shadow of nuclear war. Ottawa, it is argued, would balk at this step because the deployment of the CAST Brigade Group would entail Canada's making a provocative act, one that could itself elicit a Soviet attack on northern Norway, which in turn would trigger a war. The conclusion of this argument is that, not wishing even to contemplate having to make such a decision, Canada should abandon the CAST commitment and all efforts to make it viable.

There are two fundamental problems with this argument.

The first is that it ignores completely that the deployment
of reinforcements during a crisis is supposed to include an
element of provocation. It is meant to signal the allied determination to defend the entire NATO perimeter. If war does
break out, it is meant to ensure that the alliance would be
in a better position to sustain resistance. The element of pro-
vocativeness is inherent in the increased military effectiveness. The hope, of course, would be that this particular
show of resolve, as well as the myriad other essentially defensive steps NATO would undertake during a period of strategic warning, would dissuade the Soviets from actually attack-
ing. This can only be a hope. The alternative is to do nothing
during the warning time and thus be prepared either to give
in before the shooting starts, lose quickly, or escalate immediately to nuclear weapons.

Were Canada to abandon the CAST commitment on the
grounds that a crisis deployment would be too provocative
an action for it to consider, Ottawa would in effect be in-
dicating a willingness to accept a priori one of these alternatives. It would certainly reflect poorly on Canada's supposed commitment to collective deterrence.

The second problem with the argument is that it implies
that the decision to send the CAST Brigade Group would be
taken in a vacuum, that the eyes of the world would be fixed
solely on the territory of northern Norway, and that the
Soviets would be so provoked that they would move from
crisis to World War III. Yet probably the circumstances
under which NATO would request deployment of the CAST
force would be those in which a host of other reinforcement
efforts would already be under way. Canada's allies would be
in various states of mobilization with ships moving toward
Norway, aircraft undertaking extensive surveillance, and
ground forces being brought up to strength throughout
NATO Europe and the United States. In fact, Ottawa would
never decide to dispatch the CAST force unless it was acting
at the specific request of its allies and most likely in conjunction with similar allied efforts. To be sure, the decision would
nonetheless be a fateful and difficult one. But it would not
be one that Canada would take alone.

Canadian Forces Europe

Even though it constitutes a standing force, the role of the
4CMBG is militarily far less important than the CAST Brigade Group. Although it is located on the vital central front,
its 77 Leopard tanks, 3,200 troops, and the reinforcements
from Canada it would receive make an insignificant contribution to the 2 million men that SACEUR would have at his
disposal. Even if the 4CMBG's numbers were doubled, or if
it, as has sometimes been proposed, were joined by a second
brigade group—both dubious propositions given the capital
shortages the Canadian Armed Forces are facing and the personnel shortage in the FMC—the balance on the central front
would hardly be affected. Canada will have enough troubles
trying to keep the Brigade Group equipped to meet the chang-
ing tactical environment there. From time to time, proposals
are made in Canada to have the Brigade Group shed its armor and assume a very light role as commando or harass-
ment troops. The impulse behind these suggestions may be
commendable, but they would only have the effect of render-
ing an insignificant force still more insignificant simply to
preserve for political reasons some Canadian land presence
in West Germany. It would become tokenism in the extreme.

   The 4CMBG is a puny commitment and deserves to be
treated as such. NATO has a strong military incentive to encourage Canada to emphasize its assets: to concentrate on
the CAST commitment and to dissolve the 4CMBG. The two
steps are complementary. Much of the equipment that would
have to be transported by sea to Norway for the CAST
Brigade Group is now located in parallel stocks at the Canadian Forces Base at Lahr, West Germany, the 4CMBG's
home. This includes such major weapon systems as armored
personnel carriers, armored reconnaissance vehicles, self-
propelled howitzers, and even helicopters. It will eventually include elements of the low-level air defense system. This
is all equipment that, upon termination of the Canadian land
presence on the central front, could be moved from West Germany and pre-positioned in Norway for the CAST Brigade
Group.

Along with the West German commitment, the FMC would shed its heavy armored role entirely – and with it the Leopard tanks. Canadian tanks in West Germany could be turned over to the Germans – and so could the Canadian tanks in Canada. In still another of the ironies surrounding the Canadian Armed Forces, there are often more West German tanks in Canada training with the West German armed forces, the *Bundeswehr*, in Shilo, Manitoba, than the FMC has across Canada. The savings here would be substantial. Canada would avoid the major new investments that will be required to keep its heavy armored role viable, and the FMC would no longer have to be prepared to reinforce both a heavy armored central front commitment and the more lightly armed forces in Norway. From that point of view alone, the 4CMBG is not a viable commitment: it is a nuisance. Finally, with the dissolution of the 4CMBG, Canadian airlift capabilities could be exclusively directed to the northern flank. Those capabilities currently have to be divided between Norway and West Germany.

The 54 CF-18 interceptors that the 1CAG will be deploying in West Germany are undeniably an improvement over the ancient Starfighters. But they also constitute but a tiny contribution to the fighters that SACEUR would have at his disposal. If the 1CAG were also dissolved, as it should be, the aircraft could be brought home to Canada not only to fill the gaps in North America, but to guarantee that Canada's other commitment to the northern flank, that of providing aircraft, becomes credible. AIRCOM is worried that the 138 CF-18s will not be sufficient for North America, West Germany, and Norway, especially now that the government has let the option to buy an additional 20 planes pass. With the substantial savings that would accrue from shedding the armored role and closing down the expensive Canadian facilities in West Germany (coupled with increases in the defense budget), the government could then consider the modest expansion of the CAST force to 5,000 or perhaps 6,000 and the acquisition of three desperately needed systems: more airlift capability for the CAST Brigade Group,

AWACS aircraft for the surveillance of southern Canadian airspace, and more maritime forces.

Maritime Command

The bleak prospects for significant numerical increases in Canada's maritime forces should also be of concern to the United States and its NATO allies. NATO is, after all, as much a maritime alliance as it is a compact to ensure the territorial integrity of its West European members. Indeed, precisely because of NATO's "continentalist" emphasis, it has long been concerned with security in the Atlantic Ocean and the Mediterranean. Maritime forces constitute parts of the alliance's triad of strategic nuclear, theater-tactical nuclear, and, above all, conventional postures. NATO maritime forces would seek to secure and exploit the strategic value of the seas for the traditional purposes of conveyance and the projection of force ashore.

Since the beginning of allied maritime planning in 1949 and the creation of the position of Supreme Allied Commander Atlantic (SACLANT) in 1952, Canada has postured the bulk of its maritime forces to contribute to the NATO ASW effort. In particular, Canada has assumed the responsibility for providing the alliance with surface ships for convoy escort. The Defence Department itself stresses that the decision not to live up to the 1977 goals for MARCOM, "fails to address the shortfall of surface combatants that has been the most critical deficiency of NATO's maritime forces." For this reason, the department assigned "the highest priority to seeking approval for a follow-on contract" for a second batch of six frigates."[24]

That shortfall is indeed critical. Today, the alliance can count on roughly 170 non-U.S. escort ships with sufficiently modern capabilities. But many of these forces will be dedicated to other tasks in the event of war. For example, the West German and Danish forces will have to patrol the Baltic exits and may be required in the North Sea. Norwegian forces will have as an immediate task conducting operations along the northern flank, while the British Royal Navy will be deployed in the English Channel and along the GIUK gap. Projected building and retirement rates for non-U.S. surface escorts indicate a less than one-for-one replacement during this decade. Thus, as the U.S. Congressional Budget Office concluded, " . . . U.S. defensive forces – already required for protection of U.S. carrier task forces, underway replenishment groups, amphibious groups and perhaps convoys to Asia – could also be required for transatlantic convoy escort."[25]

There is no certainty that the U.S. Navy will be able to compensate for the shortfall in NATO convoy escorts. The opportunity exists, therefore, for Canada to make a significant contribution to collective security by expanding its surface fleet. Given that the bulk of other allied escort forces will be occupied in the eastern Atlantic and coastal seas, even a force of 12 CPFs and 4 Tribal class destroyers would make a measurable contribution to the allied escort effort, provided all 16 were deployed to the Atlantic. If Canada is going to continue to deploy ships on both coasts, even more surface escorts will be needed.

In addition to surface escorts, NATO would also benefit from more Canadian LRPAs. In its recommendations, the Canadian Senate committee called for a doubling of the Aurora force to 36. Not only would this enhance Canada's capabilities in the western Atlantic, it could also allow MARCOM to make available LRPAs to support NATO in the central and eastern ocean regions.

There are two other general roles for Canada's maritime forces whose fulfillment is now also in serious doubt as a result of the present condition and future prospects for MARCOM. These are, first, the seaward defense of North America, and, second, the protection of Canadian sovereignty.

In cooperation with the U.S. Navy, Canada has long provided forces for the surveillance of continental waters against intrusion by Soviet submarines, both attack and ballistic missile. Although it is certainly the case that the Soviet Union can strike at North American targets from submarines

located near the USSR itself, both Canada and the United
States have regarded the possibility of close-in low trajec-
tory launches of shorter-range ballistic missiles as a threat.
With the expected increases in Soviet sea-launched cruise
missile (SLCM) capabilities, there is an added requirement
for seaward surveillance. Also of concern are Soviet attack
submarines that might threaten the U.S. Trident fleet near
their bases on the Pacific and Atlantic coasts.

In the coming years, the polar regions will probably become an increasingly important area of deployment for Soviet
submarines as they seek safer waters. The U.S. Navy does
envision, in the event of war, the use of its attack submarines
for ASW operations against the Soviet fleet, which may ne-
cessitate greater under-ice capability. The Soviets may attempt to transit their attack submarines under the polar ice
cap to outflank NATO ASW barriers in the eastern Atlantic and Norwegian seas. This would allow them to emerge
near the main shipping lanes.

MARCOM has no under-ice capability, and the ability
of its forces to operate in the Arctic is quite limited. Here,
as in the other seaward approaches to the continent, it is important that both the United States and Canada know as
much as possible about what is going on. But, as in the case
of Canada's commitment to NATO's maritime posture, MAR-
COM's ability to contribute to the seaward defense of North
America is declining. The lack of adequate surface forces and
the small number of LRPAs is relevant to the North American as well as to the NATO role. In the North American case,
however, the problem is compounded by the virtual lack of
effective submarine forces and Arctic waters capabilities. Unless improvements are made, the U.S. Navy might well have
to undertake a greater measure of surveillance activities within or near Canadian waters. Such activities, when revealed
or suspected, bring forth cries of protest in Canada. Some
Canadians regard U.S. efforts to keep watch on Soviet submarine movements more of a threat to Canadian sovereignty than the Soviet activities themselves. It is unlikely that
U.S. Navy forces would enter Canadian waters without MAR-

COM's knowledge. No doubt MARCOM finds this more of an affront to its honor than a threat to Canadian sovereignty. After all, the U.S. Navy is only doing the job MARCOM is supposed to do.

As to MARCOM's role in the protection of Canadian sovereignty from nonmilitary threats such as illegal fishing and environmental pollution at sea, Canada is certainly justified in ensuring that its maritime forces provide a backup to the civil authority. Just as AIRCOM ought to be able to deal with stray aircraft, so too should MARCOM have the capability to identify and, if necessary, apprehend ships violating Canadian sovereignty knowingly or unknowingly. Contrary to the implications of the 1971 white paper, however, there is really no reason to believe that Canada's alliance obligations prevent its maritime forces (and, indeed, its air forces) from fulfilling a sovereignty protection role. A MARCOM that is in a position to contribute credibly to NATO and to the defense of North America would have more than enough resources to deal with sovereignty threats that the civilian agencies, such as the Coast Guard, could not cope with. Moreover, what better demonstration is there of the seriousness with which Canada takes its sovereignty protection than the maintenance of adequate maritime forces?

Given that force building to meet the NATO and North American roles should determine MARCOM's posture, what should Canada do to improve its maritime forces? If funds were unlimited, the force posture recommended by the Senate committee in 1983, namely a fleet consisting of 16 surface ships, 20 submarines, 36 Auroras, as well as minesweepers and fast patrol boats, might be adopted. But the money is not there. Even with major increases in overall defense expenditures, in particular for the funding of maritime forces, the Senate posture could not be achieved. A more modest approach is realistic. For the NATO and North American roles, MARCOM needs more surface ships of the CPF type, more LRPAs, and modern submarines. A minimum of 12 (but ideally 18) CPFs, 36 Auroras, and 10 submarines would be required. A further and most useful step would be to station only two surface ships on the west coast, concentrating the rest in the east where they could contribute significantly to the NATO escort posture. An escort capability is not required on the west coast, where Canada has no transoceanic security commitments. The west coast North American defense roles could be assumed by LRPAs and submarines. For the Arctic roles, new submarines should have full under-ice capability. In addition, Canada should consider deploying underwater sensor arrays at key points in the Arctic.

Bringing MARCOM up to a credible stature will thus enhance security on both sides of the Atlantic. Canada is uniquely suited to support its allies at sea through an expansion of its maritime forces. At sea, the relative importance of significant increases in Canadian force building would be great. Ten modern attack submarines and 12 or more additional escort ships would augment the West's collective forces much more than bringing the forces in Europe up to currently stated wartime levels.

A Distinctive Contribution

In short, Canada has substantial strategic assets that it can bring to NATO, namely an expertise in winter warfare, which is of great value on the northern flank, and an ideal location and a naval tradition, which permit it to contribute substantially to NATO forces at sea. Something needs to give, though, and the most logical candidates are the militarily least important contributions, the 4CMBG and the 1CAG, which constitute CFE.

The restructuring of Canada's defense posture to include a withdrawal from the central front is by no means predicated on the notion that the central front is or will become less crucial to Western security. There is little doubt that this region will remain the most important allied perimeter, militarily and politically. But the importance of the central front to NATO does not mean that any Canadian contribution to the allied posture there is of value, no matter how small. Quite simply, if that contribution does nothing to augment NATO's military situation, then maintaining it betokens a lack of appreciation for the importance of the region rather than a desire to strengthen it.

There is, of course, the argument that since the central front is so important, a restructured Canadian defense posture should emphasize this role rather than the Norwegian and maritime roles. According to that argument, Canada's NATO expenditures should be used to bring the 4CMBG and the 1CAG up to credible levels. But what would those levels be? The 4CMBG would have to be replaced with a force of divisional strength, including some 16 thousand troops and commensurate increases in armor and antiarmor capability. As for airpower, there would need to be a doubling of the existing force of 54 planes. The difficulties in implementing such an approach are overwhelming. Canada is already short of CF-18s. Many more would have to be purchased. Manpower levels would have to be increased dramatically, almost doubling the number of army personnel. Equipment costs would be staggering, and such a large European force would require more base and support facilities, adding still more heavy costs.

Most important, though, for Canada to attempt to bring its European forces up to these levels it would have to eliminate the Norwegian commitment and curtail maritime forces to such an extent that MARCOM would be of even less use to NATO than it now is. Some other country would have to make up the difference in Norway, and the U.S. Navy would have to try to assume some former Canadian roles at sea. It is hard to see how the alliance would benefit from that situation. On the other hand, a withdrawal of Canadian forces from West Germany would not result in any significant gaps, for those forces make but an insignificant contribution. In sum, Canada's role in West Germany is the most expendable for NATO, while the Norwegian and maritime roles are the least.

Some Canadians, greatly concerned about the commitment-capability gap, have suggested that the restructuring of Canada's NATO commitments could be achieved without withdrawing from the politically important West German role. One variant would have the air group alone brought back to Canada while the ground forces currently located in Canada, but dedicated to the reinforcement of Norway, would join the 4CMBG in West Germany. Still another suggestion would include the abandonment of the Canadian presence in Germany but substitute a Scottish presence, whereby forces dedicated to Norway would be closer to their reinforcement destination on the northern flank.

But these suggestions also have their drawbacks and fail to address the fundamental burdens caused by fragmentation. In the first place, with greater pre-positioning of equipment and adequate air transport there is no reason for the Norwegian reinforcement units to be stationed in Europe. Unless the air transport units were to be permanently stationed in Europe as well, sitting on the runway there for immediate use, there would be little time gained in keeping the ground forces units in either West Germany or Scotland.

Second, in the case of maintaining the ground forces in West Germany, it does not seem wise for Canada to place troops near the central front if it expects that they will be used elsewhere. The only reason Canada would maintain reinforcement units in West Germany would be for the traditional political reasons – demonstrating solidarity with the allies, especially the West Germans. The importance of a physical presence in West Germany to serve this end will be discussed in the concluding chapter. Suffice it to say here that it stretches political rationality to the limit to have troops destined for other locations stationed in West Germany when they could do the job just as well by remaining in Canada.

Third, these suggestions would still entail the expenses of foreign basing. Indeed, because the transport aircraft would have to be located with the ground units, even greater expenses would be incurred. There would be less saving from the withdrawal of the 1CAG, and Canada would still need air bases in West Germany. Moreover, the transports once stationed in Europe would be unavailable in peacetime for use in Canada for the routine air movement of forces and Defence Department personnel.

Finally, since there would be little real savings, Canada would still face underfunding of its other defense roles. Like the suggestion that CFE be given priority in terms of defense expenditures, these variants of restructuring would all entail continued fragmentation to the detriment of both Canada and its allies.

Canada needs to emphasize its defense assets as part of a restructuring of the Canadian Armed Forces not only for the immediate value of those assets to the alliance, but also for their impact at home. There has been a divided and dissipated character to Canada's military efforts. This has only served to strengthen public doubts about the country's ability to contribute to collective security. It is obvious to Canadians that their fragmented forces constitute nothing more than a Lilliputian facsimile of the commitments of the U.S. Armed Forces, contributing little to any of the military subbalances that constitute the overall East-West balance. A restructuring of the forces to emphasize Canadian assets would give them a distinct character and a distinct role that Canadians could recognize – and perhaps even identify with. In a country constantly in search of an elusive national identity and a role in world affairs such forces could become, far from the butt of humor, a source of national distinctiveness and pride.

4

Toward a New Canadian Defense Posture: Imperatives for Change and Leadership

The decision of the Mulroney government to spend no more than 2.1 percent of its GNP on national defense and to leave the Canadian Armed Forces fragmented should not go unchallenged by Canada's allies. But the allies should also be prepared to offer encouragement to Ottawa if the white paper on defense to be issued by Erik Nielsen points out a new direction in which Canada emphasizes its military assets.

The temptation will no doubt be very strong in the other NATO capitals to take whatever Ottawa offers. Washington and Brussels may be coming to the conclusion that they should simply accept anything they get from Canada, given the country's recent history and given the absence of direct U.S. leverage over the level of Canadian defense expenditures. Certainly Ottawa is counting on just that kind of reaction from its NATO partners.

But by giving in to such a temptation, Canada's allies will all but ensure the perpetuation of the fragmentation of the Canadian contribution to collective security. The alliance itself shares a measure of responsibility for the present state of Canada's armed forces. After all, Canada's contributions have been made for political purposes – in essence to please the allies. They have been allowed to decay to token levels as Ottawa calculated that such tokens were all that were

needed to keep its seat at NATO's table. The allies have acquiesced. Although Canada's reputation in Brussels may be
tarnished and its military personnel embarrassed, it has been
permitted to remain a member of the Western alliance in good
political standing. NATO has the Canadian commitment it
deserves.

The allies have gone along with the Canadian air and
ground forces contribution in West Germany for 30 years,
although it has been nearly 20 years since those forces have
been of value to the allied posture along the central front.
When Trudeau cut Canada's European forces in half in 1969,
the allies briefly protested, but there was no concerted effort
to trade a reduction in these forces for increases in other commitments. NATO then acquiesced in a new Canadian commitment to Norway, even though it was clear that Canada
had neither then, nor subsequently, the capacity to reinforce
the northern flank in a timely or effective manner. To permit this weak reinforcement commitment was particularly
surprising because during the 1970s the northern flank
assumed increasing importance in NATO calculations as ex-
emplified by a new, major commitment of U.S. Marines to
reinforce the area. Thus today the alliance has token Canadian commitments to both West Germany and Norway.

At sea, the alliance has been facing a dramatic rise in
Soviet maritime capabilities, which, along with the strategy
of flexible response, has generated greater demands for the
kinds of ASW forces Canada could supply. Since the 1970s,
however, Canada's maritime forces have declined at an even
faster pace than its land and air forces, to the point at which
under existing plans MARCOM will have only 10 NATO
class warships by the mid-1990s. And yet Canada has remained an active participant in Allied Command Atlantic
(ACLANT), sailing proudly with the Standing Naval Force
Atlantic (STANAVFORLANT).

The United States bears a special measure of responsibility for the fragmented condition of the Canadian Armed
Forces. Although the United States has, with justification,

wanted Canada to contribute to both NATO and NORAD, it has rarely considered how Canada could best make a valuable contribution to both. This was acceptable when the air defense of North America was not a priority for the United States. Since 1980, however, the United States itself has placed more emphasis on improving warning of and defense against a direct attack on North America by air and sea. In the next decade this will require greater expenditure by Canada if the nation is to continue to contribute not only to the defense of the continent but also to enforce its own sovereignty.

Unfortunately, though, Washington appears just as anxious that Canada maintain and improve its fragmented and marginal commitments to NATO. There has been no indication from the U.S. government that Canada should continue to contribute to collective defense in any other way than it has done in the past or that the fragmentation of the Canadian contribution is of concern to the United States. This was reaffirmed at the highest level when President Reagan and Prime Minister Mulroney issued their joint declaration on security at the Quebec summit. In it they reiterated "our determination to continue substantial real growth in expenditures for defence," a formula tailored to justify Canada's low defense spending by emphasizing real growth rates rather than the percentage of GNP. They also said "We attach great importance to our continuing commitment to station Canadian and United States forces in Europe," making a comparison between the Canadian token and the real U.S. contribution. What appeared to be a pledge opening a new era in bilateral defense cooperation was in fact a continuation of the existing Canadian defense posture, which will add less and less to the U.S. global posture in the coming years. In fairness, it should be added that the declaration was issued in the heady days before the May 1985 budget (much less the February 1986 budget), at a time when it appeared that the Mulroney government might be serious about defense after all.

Urging Canada to Emphasize Its Assets

As argued in chapter 3, for Canada to make the real contribution to collective security of which it is eminently capable, it will have to emphasize its military assets. Even if increases in Canadian defense spending were doubled, now an impossibility in the wake of the February 1986 budget, Canada would still not have sufficient resources to bring all of its fragmented commitments up to a level at which they could make more than token contributions. This restructuring would entail the following elements:

1. An increase in maritime forces based on the acquisition of at least 12, and ideally more, CPFs, as well as submarines and more LRPAs.
2. An increase in resources for North American defense, in particular the deployment of more CF-18s and the acquisition of radar coverage for the hole in the Canadian south.
3. Enhancement of the commitment to reinforce Norway, accomplished through more extensive pre-positioning of Canadian military equipment in Norway, the acquisition of better airlift capability, and the deployment of a greater number of CF-18s in Canada, ready to be flown to Norway.
4. Termination of the Canadian military presence on the central front.

This restructuring is predicated upon increases in Canada's overall defense expenditures occurring simultaneously. This would mean that any increases would go to strengthening those roles for which Canada is better suited. A simple pullout from West Germany, with a redistribution of existing, or marginally greater, resources to the other roles, would not have much of an impact. It would simply be a shell game that would meet neither Canadian nor allied needs. Manageable increases, however, if properly directed, could afford Canada the opportunity to rebuild its armed forces so that they would make a valuable contribution to both allied and Canadian security.

Restructuring would be a long-term process taking 5 to 10 years. As Canada builds up its maritime forces, its air defense forces, and its Norwegian reinforcement capabilities, the forces in Europe would remain in place, but would not be equipped with new major weapon systems. Once the capabilities for meeting other roles appeared to be well under way, the forces in Europe could be withdrawn.

For restructuring to occur, the NATO allies would have to play a fundamental role. They would need to provide Canada with the political encouragement required to undertake such a bold initiative. The current situation is largely the result of past Canadian governments' attempting to solidify political ties with NATO allies, especially in the case of West Germany. Only a green light from NATO can persuade Ottawa that everyone will benefit if increases in Canadian defense expenditures are directed toward reduced commitments.

It is on this question of allied acquiescence that objections are frequently raised to the restructuring of Canada's contributions to include a withdrawal from the central front. There are three major objections.

First, it is argued that a withdrawal from Europe, even if undertaken in the context of increased Canadian defense expenditures and an augmentation of other roles, will undermine Canada's ties with NATO and signal a retreat from collective security. This objection is important, but not sustainable in the long run. It is based on the belief that it is the physical presence of Canadian forces in West Germany that ties Canada to NATO. But it has been Canada that has maintained that its small force is the proof of its commitment. The Europeans have accepted this and have therefore encouraged Canada to continue the commitment despite its lack of military importance. This, in turn, has caused Ottawa to brush aside suggestions for withdrawal and concentration on other allied tasks—because the Europeans, above all the West Germans, would not stand for it.

Yet Canada's interest in collective defense through NATO is much deeper than the presence of a small token force in West Germany would indicate. Canada's ties to the alliance are based on a common strategic outlook that it shares with the United States and that holds that Europe is the most important military region in the world. Canada promoted the creation of NATO before there was any suggestion that Canadian troops had to be stationed abroad and would remain in Europe for 30 years.

Of equal importance, West Germany's interest in Canadian commitment deals with those elements that would em-political symbol. West German security rests in part on a secure northern flank and open sea-lanes across which reinforcements could come. To the extent Canada makes real contributions to NATO efforts in those two areas, it makes real contributions to German security.

The second objection to the restructuring of the Canadian commitment deals with those elements that would emphasize the growing importance of North American air defense: If Canada augments its North American forces in response to new U.S. priorities, it would further undermine the alliance by drawing more sharply the division between U.S. and European interests. Superficially this objection seems plausible and is only partially mitigated by the fact that by removing the CF-18s from Germany, Canada would increase its ability to send aircraft to Norway in the event of an emergency. U.S. and Canadian concerns over new threats to North America are legitimate, however, and the Europeans can hardly expect the two countries to forgo improvements in their joint defense efforts. There will always be a measure of uncertainty as to how closely the U.S. ties its own security to that of the Europeans, but European security will certainly not be enhanced if the United States perceives itself to be without adequate warning, surveillance, and bomber defense forces. This is apart from the fact that many of the improvements in North America relate to the global U.S. strategic nuclear posture upon which the Europeans ultimately rely for their security.

Canada also has legitimate specific national interests in improving its capability to monitor its own airspace, including the plugging of the hole in the south. It can undertake this alone or, more likely, in conjunction with the United States through NORAD, or, as suggested in chapter 3, simply in cooperation with the United States without the joint NORAD command structure. Moreover, because the United States is moving ahead with improvements to continental defense, Canada has the choice of either accepting the U.S. invitation to continued cooperation or allowing continental air defense to become increasingly a U.S. operation. Surely, NATO cannot expect Ottawa to allow the United States to move unilaterally in North America so that Canada can maintain its military insignificant air defense role in Europe. For that reason, all of Canada's CF-18s are best located in Canada.

The third objection is the most serious. If Canada is allowed to restructure its contributions, other NATO allies, including perhaps the United States, might be tempted to do the same. This is the so-called slippery-slope argument. It has less to do with Canada's role in the alliance or the effect on NATO of Canada's withdrawal from West Germany than it has with the precedent that might be set.

Although it would certainly be harmful to the alliance, and to Canada, if other allies restructured their commitments, there is no reason to hold that this would inevitably follow from any Canadian force structure decision. Canadian actions are rarely followed by other alliance members when making their own decisions. But it is surprising how influential Canada suddenly seems whenever suggestions are made for a change in Canada's contribution. The reality is that other NATO members do not take their cue from Ottawa. Nor should they.

There is little reason why it cannot be made clear that the restructuring of Canada's commitments would be in response to Canada's unique position. Canada is not a European country and it does have obligations to collective security in North America. Moreover, by restructuring its contributions, Canada would be able to make its other contributions of value to NATO and the United States. Any Europeans who might be tempted to restructure their own commitments would largely be withdrawing from some significant alliance roles to bolster other areas.

As to the impact of a Canadian withdrawl on the U.S. presence in Germany, here again, objections seem to rest on results that need not necessarily follow. The relationship of U.S. conventional forces in Europe to NATO's overall posture is of an entirely different order than that of Canadian forces. U.S. forces provide a substantial contribution to SACEUR's available forces and are also the indispensable link between U.S. and European security. There is pressure within the Congress to reduce the size of the U.S. forces unless the Europeans spend more on defense, and some in Congress might seize upon a Canadian decision to pull out of Germany to support this call. If, however, the U.S. Defense and State Departments, along with the European allies, showed that Canada was only withdrawing from West Germany to make more valuable contributions elsewhere, involving substantial increases in Canadian defense spending, this pretext could be refuted. A restructured Canadian contribution would signal a recommitment by Canada to NATO, and, far from setting a bad example, the steps undertaken would demonstrate how seriously Canada takes its allied obligations and how important Ottawa believes collective security is for Canada.

A Carrot for Canada—and a Stick

Because a restructured Canadian commitment to collective security, accompanied by significant increases in defense spending, would enhance rather than detract from the security of the alliance, Canada's allies ought to play an important role in supporting such a move by Ottawa. It would be far more preferable, however, if the first step were to be taken by the Canadian government.

It is at this stage that the allies should make it clear publicly that they are prepared to accommodate the restructuring of Canada's contributions to collective security if this takes place simultaneously with significant increases in defense expenditure. Indeed, because across-the-board increases alone will not help the allies, the allies should openly state their preference for a restructured Canadian commitment. The only Canadian policy that would be more preferable to a restructuring would be extraordinary increases in Canadian defense spending, of such a magnitude that Canada could make all of its commitments significant. This would involve deploying a division-strength armored force in West Germany with twice the number of fighter aircraft located there, as well as a 18-ship modern navy, a CAST Brigade Group provided with both adequate air transport and pre-positioned equipment in Norway, and increased air defense forces in Canada, most notably more CF-18s and AWACS aircraft. But this is a step Ottawa is in no position to take at this time.

Of particular importance in the effort will be allied statements that reassure Canada that its political ties to NATO will not in any way be affected by the restructuring of its contributions. Here it is the West German government that ought to play a leading role. This would begin with an endorsement of the Canadian initiative by the chancellor himself, emphasizing that West Germany welcomed the new contributions to West German security that Canada would be making at sea and on the northern flank.

Another element of the NATO response could be a proposal to establish within NATO a northern working group composed of Canada, Norway, the United Kingdom, Iceland, Denmark, and perhaps the United States. The group, which might be dubbed "NATO-North," would meet from time to time, including at the ministerial level, to review aspects of northern air, sea, and land policies. This step would provide something of an institutional setting for the restructured Canadian commitment, which would be largely directed toward NATO's northern flank. It would also bolster the allied reassurances that Canada was to remain active in NATO councils. Indeed, Canada might be invited by the alliance to take the lead in organizing NATO-North, and a small international secretariat for the group might be located in Ottawa.

Although the European allies will be important external supporters of a restructured Canadian commitment, the United States, as alliance leader, will have to play an active role as well. This will continue to require a measure of circumspection on Washington's part. Any Canadian government will have a hard time defending changes in its defense posture that appear to be dictated by the White House, although the United States does have a real interest in a restructured Canadian defense posture that provides more resources for ACLANT, Norway, and North American air defense. The United States must therefore encourage the European allies to do their part in supporting Canada. Thus it would be best for Washington to endorse a Canadian restructuring proposal as part of a general NATO statement that would make reference to Canada's important role in North American air defense.

Beyond these public endorsements, the United States and other allies should undertake efforts to reassure the Canadian prime minister and members of the Cabinet privately of the sincerity of their support. In the case of Canadian-U.S. relations, steps should be taken to ensure that the State and Defense Department bureaucracies are brought on board. At present there is no consensus within the U.S. government on how best to restructure the Canadian contribution. The secretaries of state and defense must therefore send the word down that the United States is in favor of a Canadian withdrawal from a central front role. Key members of Congress must also be persuaded of the benefits of the approach.

It would be far preferable for the Canadian government itself to initiate a program of significantly enhanced defense spending and restructuring of its commitments. The outlook is not good, however. With its May 1985 budget, the Progressive Conservative government set out on a course that will not take defense spending above 2.1 percent of the GNP. The Tories have also reaffirmed in one way or another all of the existing fragmented commitments. The Quebec declaration asserted their interest in keeping CFE, and Erik

Nielsen announced that CFE troop strength will be increased by 1,200. Shipbuilding continues. The CAST Brigade Group will be test deployed. North American air defense is being improved. Although surprises are always possible, the defense white paper that Nielsen is expected to issue early in 1986 will in all probability simply reconfirm all existing involvements and hold out nothing more than the vaguest of hopes that someday defense spending will be significantly increased.

If this in fact turns out to be the case, the United States and the other NATO allies must be prepared to raise the possibility that Canada will pay penalties in the immediate future unless it does something about the state of its defense posture, beyond the marginal improvements ordered by the Mulroney government. Canadian defenses have sunk to their present state in part because the Canadian government was never threatened with allied retaliation. Canadian military leaders attending allied meetings may have felt a little uncomfortable, but Liberal governments of the 1960s and 1970s were not much concerned about this because Canada was still an active member of NATO's civilian and military institutions. Canadian cabinet ministers, diplomats, and senior officers continued to participate in the whole spectrum of intra-alliance politics and consultation. Indeed, a Canadian admiral was made chairman of the NATO Military Committee.

The alliance, however, should now discuss means of persuading Canada either to bring all its commitments up to military effectiveness, or, more preferably and more feasibly, restructure those commitments as part of a sustained, though less dramatic, increase in defense expenditures. The most effective way to exercise such persuasion would be to restrict Canadian participation within NATO and NATO-related activities. As a signatory of the North Atlantic Treaty, Canada has the legitimate right to a seat at the North Atlantic Council, but other options remain:

• The members of the alliance could issue a public statement regretting that Canada, one of the founding members, was failing to carry its fair share of the collective burden.

• The Canadian representatives could be formally requested to cease attending meetings of the Defense Planning Committee and the Nuclear Planning Group.

• Canada could be asked to reduce its military personnel at the NATO military headquarters and civilian personnel at NATO political headquarters.

• Canada could be called on to withdraw from certain cooperative armaments efforts such as the frigate programs.

• Canadian participation in joint military exercises could be curtailed and Canada requested to remove its ships from STANAVFORLANT.

• Finally, Canada could be temporarily excluded from certain allied consultations, held on the staff levels, concerning such issues as the strategic arms control and Mutual and Balanced Force Reduction (MBFR) talks.

All of these steps could at first simply be raised with Ottawa as possibilities. They might also be first discussed by members of U.S. Congress as a parallel step to the Nunn amendment. Even the suggestion that restrictions would be placed on Canadian participation would be something of a shock to Ottawa and the Canadian people, who have been allowed to believe that whatever the level of Canadian defense spending, Canadians were welcome in Brussels.

Some would argue that if NATO can live with such crises as the Greek-Turkish dispute and not ask Greek or Turkish diplomats or soldiers to restrict their participation in allied councils, surely it can accommodate Canada's defense posture. After all, Canada remains a loyal member of the alliance and has supported every major allied decision from flexible response to the INF approach. Moreover, if NATO starts singling out members for deficiencies in defense spending, where will it end?

These concerns are valid. But, here again, reference must be made to Canada's unique place within the Western alliance system. Part of that uniqueness is that Canada needs its allies more than they need Canada. Because both Greece and

Turkey hold key geographic positions in Europe, NATO is compelled to bend to maintain their active participation in the alliance. Although the alliance must do what it can to maintain Canadian participation, there is not the same relevance as in the case of even small European members. It is, for example, more crucial that Belgium hold to its commitment to allow deployment of nuclear weapons on its soil than it is to have Canada as a member of the Nuclear Planning Group.

As to the danger of singling out a particular member of the alliance for spending deficiencies, here the Europeans could counter that they have always been subject to such criticism from Washington—especially from members of the U.S. Congress. Indeed, the only country that seems to escape such criticism is Canada. If the United States can threaten the Europeans with pullbacks of U.S. troops to persuade them to maintain their capabilities, certainly the Europeans can suggest that unless Canada does more to maintain allied capabilities restrictions will be put on its NATO participation. In a sense, by raising the possibility of imposing penalties, the Europeans would be compensating for the lack of leverage Washington possesses.

Canadians may well question whether such threats might not be a challenge to Canada's sovereignty. Would not bending to them do more to damage Canadian prestige than the continued maintenance of the existing defense posture? Allied threats could fuel the argument for Canadian withdrawal from its security pacts, and some would see the not-so-hidden hand of Washington behind the NATO moves, encouraging nationalist, anti-American sentiment.

All this is a possibility and entails the risk that, if the domestic reaction in Canada were overwhelming, the country might decide to withdraw from NATO. That would indeed be unfortunate because Canada is eminently capable of making significant contributions to the defense of the West. NATO does need Canada, but in the final analysis. Canada needs NATO even more. It cannot afford to leave the alliance. As has been recognized by every single Canadian government

since 1949, membership in the alliance is a cornerstone of
Canadian involvement in world affairs. It provides the Canadian government entry to the great strategic decisions affecting the East-West balance, and it provides Ottawa with a dip-
lomatic and even psychological counterweight to what might
otherwise be the stifling embrace of the superpower to the
south. Ultimately, though, Canada is a Western nation whose
security interests lie with the West. As the Mulroney government itself recently recognized in its green paper on foreign
policy:

> . . . there has never been any serious question of our
> adopting a neutral position between East and West. We
> are determined to uphold and defend our ideals of free-
> dom and democracy. The Soviet Union is a formidable,
> conventionally armed and nuclear-armed adversary.
> The need to defend ourselves is real. Hence our mem-
> bership in NATO and our cooperation with the United
> States in the defence of North America.[26]

Moreover, NATO members need not discuss the issue of
sanctions from a position of hostility, much less vindictive-
ness. Making Canadian defense efforts significant serves the
interests of NATO and of Canada itself. The withdrawal from
a central front role would make available more forces in Canada while avoiding the cost of foreign basing. Emphasis on
air defense and maritime forces would provide augmented capabilities for the assertion of Canadian sovereignty in North
America. Making the Norwegian reinforcement commitment
the main task of Canada's ground forces would provide them
with a much more important and distinct role than that of
a reserve task force in West Germany. In sum, the allies will
be presenting to Canada an offer that should be hard to re-
fuse, saying, in effect, "We will support you in making your
contribution to collective security better suited to your unique
position and national needs and in such a way enhance our
mutual security. If you are unwilling to take this step, we
may be compelled to place some restrictions upon your participation within your alliances."

Leadership from Ottawa

It would take a large measure of leadership on the part of Canada's new Conservative government to implement the necessary changes in Canada's defense posture and to justify the expense to the Canadian people – with or without prompting from its NATO partners.

Of late, opponents to Canada's continued adherence to both NATO and NORAD have become more vocal. Peace groups and disarmament advocates have called not only for a greater Canadian effort to reduce the growth of superpower nuclear arsenals, but also have argued that continued membership in U.S.-led security pacts inhibits Canada from taking a distinct stand against U.S. policies. The national leadership of the recently defeated Liberal Party has been sharply critical of the Conservatives' efforts to restore confidence in Canadian-U.S. relations, focusing its attention on the dangers of SDI involvement through an unrestricted renewal of the NORAD agreement. John Turner, the leader of the Liberal Party and prime minister of Canada during the summer of 1984 until his defeat at the polls, has failed to restrain vociferous members of his caucus from making the attacks that have thus far so badly muddied the defense debate in Canada. The Liberals have been joined in their efforts by the small NDP. The New Democrats have never greatly favored NORAD and have recently reaffirmed their position that Canada should withdraw from NATO.

It is not surprising, therefore, that the Conservative government seems hesitant about major policy initiatives with regard to defense and tempted to maintain the status quo quietly. Were it to propose a review of existing allied commitments with the view toward eliminating some and strengthening others, the whole issue of Canadian involvement in collective security would come before the public and occasion vigorous debate within the House of Commons.

But this is a government with the largest parliamentary majority in Canadian history. It is a government that campaigned on a pledge to restore Canada's military capabilities

and that, despite recent budget decisions, appears more dedicated to collective security than any Canadian government
in the last 20 years. If any government could initiate a restructuring of Canada's allied commitments, it is this government, and it must be prepared to open up the debate and
forcefully state its position.

Moreover, there is good reason to believe that, once
opened, the debate will strengthen the cause of restructuring to meet alliance commitments. Public opinion polls do
indicate that a majority of Canadians still appreciate the importance of collective security. What they have a hard time
believing is how Canada can make a difference and why it
should spend more on defense. In part, this view is as much
the legacy of the Liberal years as the poor condition of the
armed forces. The Liberals all but proclaimed military ir-
relevancy and then, through deliberate policy decisions,
allowed the defense posture to correspond to this view.

By basing its future defense policies on a restructured
Canadian commitment, the Conservatives could arm themselves with compelling arguments. First, they could say to
Canadians that the government takes defense seriously, so
seriously that it is prepared to change the way Canada has
approached its allied obligations. Second, the government
could present to the public a well-thought-out defense
posture, matching capabilities to commitments and tailor-
ing those commitments to meet Canada's unique place in
Western collective security. The dissipated character of Canada's armed forces would disappear. Canadians could see that
their armed forces were making real contributions at sea, on
the northern flank, and at home.

Finally, the government would be telling the people that
by so altering its defense posture, Canada can count, that
its forces can enhance collective security in selected areas of
common endeavor. The compelling argument that should be
stressed is that the balance of power between East and West
is in reality an aggregation of interlocking regional, conventional, and nuclear subbalances. A serious shift in any one
of the subbalances in favor of the Warsaw Pact could ad-

versely affect Western collective security and could contribute to the breakdown of deterrence. When directly measured against the overall balance, Canada cannot hope to make a decisive contribution. Nonetheless, there are subbalances to which Canada can make important contributions. It is, after all, a principal power and a wealthy nation. It is also a country with both highly professional armed forces and a military history replete with valiant deeds in two world wars and in Korea. It remains a persistent irony that these "unmilitary" people have several times in this century undertaken military efforts that have astounded the world — and Canadians themselves.

As NATO itself is now again emphasizing, the greater the alliance's conventional resources, the lesser the need for reliance on nuclear weapons. On this point, a certain amount of common cause can be made in Canada between those who are concerned about the disastrous shape of the Canadian Armed Forces and those who fear reliance on nuclear weaponry, a point already made by Douglas Roche, Canada's disarmament ambassador. Canada, in short, can make real and valuable contributions to the defense of Western Europe and the deterrence of war. Almost all Canadians should agree that both are in the national interest.

Some of those arguments have at times been made or alluded to by members of the Mulroney government. But the Progressive Conservatives were badly taken aback by the defense debates in which they were charged with nuclear sell out, spurious links to the SDI, and giving in to the Yanks. The Tories have also seemed at times to be almost embarrassed about collective security and uneasy about nuclear deterrence. Throughout their first year in office, they frequently sought to justify enhancements of the Canadian Armed Forces not for the sake of defense, but so that Canada's influence in arms control negotiations might be enhanced. Brian Mulroney himself stated while campaigning that improving on the "unacceptable" conditons of the armed forces "enables us to make pretty substantial strides in the area of peace negotiations."

Such an approach, though, invites more tokenism. As the new government has probably discovered by now, the size of Canada's armed forces has little to do with the ability of Ottawa to influence arms control negotiations. Those allies in Europe directly facing the Soviets and the Americans who confront the USSR all around the world will be unlikely to be swayed by Canadian views simply because Canada has more ships, more aircraft dedicated to North American air defense, and a more credible Norwegian reinforcement capability, as important as these enhanced commitments would be and as much as they undoubtedly would be appreciated.

Moreover, as the new government should have also discovered by now, there are in fact very few major issues on which Canada is not already in substantial agreement with its allies, including arms control. Too many critics in Canada interpret Canadian support of allied decisions as subservience to Washington. Unless the Progressive Conservatives were to adopt the current foreign policy agenda of the NDP, there is little scope for major and distinctive Canadian initiatives. Any Canadian government must also bear in mind that allied cohesion, in which Canada has an abiding interest, is at times a very fragile commodity, especially on nuclear issues.

As has been shown, Canada's role in allied councils is one of consensus supporter. Its diplomats generally take account of where the allied consensus is moving and work to facilitate its implementation. Canada has played and can play a moderately effective role. But it is not a role on which increases in defense expenditures and restructuring can be sold to the Canadian people. The government must stake its claim on the simple argument that these changes are in the national security interest of Canada, an interest that can only be furthered by strengthening NATO's conventional posture.

A large measure of leadership will also be required with regard to North American defense efforts. Indeed, this area is likely to be the most controversial in the coming years, particularly if Canada restructures partly in order to be able better to meet new demands in continental defense. Already, the

Mulroney government has been attacked for paying too little heed to the dangers of continued close involvement with the United States and its dangerous strategic nuclear doctrines. The old arguments about NORAD affording Canada too little influence in comparison to NATO have begun to reemerge.

In North America the Progressive Conservatives will face a number of choices. It will not simply be a matter of bringing back the air squadrons from Europe, paying less than half the cost for the North Warning System, and building a few northern operating locations. The issue of the relationship between NORAD's role and the SDI is compelling. Although improvements to Canada's air defense forces should not be held hostage to the SDI debate, some decisions regarding command arrangements will have to be made before the outcome of SDI research and development is known. The Mulroney government cannot ignore the politically sensitive nature of the command issue, just as it cannot completely give in to those who argue that because of the SDI any form of continental defense cooperation is strategically and morally flawed.

Thus the government may well have to explore alternatives to the existing arrangements while maintaining close cooperation with the United States in the area of early warning and bomber and cruise missile defense. Yet even if NORAD is dissolved and Canada is able to put some temporary distance between its own North American efforts and U.S. space operations, Ottawa will not want to foreclose completely participation in all U.S. space-based systems such as those used for surveillance of airspace. Should bomber and cruise missile detection and active defense become possible from space, Canada may well have an interest in participating in this aspect of strategic defense because detection and interception could take place over Canada. Therefore the Progressive Conservatives face the challenge of preserving their options with regard to North American arrangements, but not allowing Canada to be shut out entirely from space-based technological developments in which it may have legitimate national security and sovereignty interests. Adept handling of the whole NORAD-SDI issue will be necessary, and the Tories will have to explain their policies to the Canadian people over a chorus of opposition criticism that no doubt will border on the sensational.

Other areas of air defense also now require decisions. There is the question of Canadian air sovereignty in the south. It is soon going to be public knowledge that North Warning, while it enhances Canada's ability to know what is entering its airspace from the north, does not solve the problem of the dismantling of the CADIN-Pinetree line. Here, too, possibly heavy expenditures on such items as AWACS and more CF-18s will have to be explained.

Beyond the air defense question will be others concerning the cooperation between MARCOM and the U.S. Navy in the seaward defense of North America. Even if Canada acquires better capabilities in the form of new submarines and surveillance platforms, including those capable of operating in the Arctic, the U.S. Navy will undoubtedly want to be made aware of what is taking place in all of Canada's territorial waters. Thus, while an enhanced MARCOM will certainly improve Canada's ability to fulfill its tasks in North America and contribute to maritime sovereignty protection, the Tories will have to maintain and explain the close cooperation between MARCOM and the U.S. Navy.

For North American roles, as for NATO roles, the restructured Canadian defense posture and attendant increases in defense expenditures would have to be presented to the Canadian people largely in terms of the relationship of these measures to collective defense, nuclear as well as conventional. For all of this, leadership from Ottawa, indeed from the prime minister, will be essential, and the task will not be an easy one.

The Tories must weigh the difficulty of their task against the problems inherent in a continuation of the present course. Without restructuring and increases in defense expenditures, Canada's armed forces will continue to decline and be all but useless to the country. As the Senate committee noted, just with regard to the maritime forces, "MARCOM, which is responsible for the country's seaward defenses, cannot meet its commitments to the protection of Canadian sovereignty, to the defense of North America—much less to NATO." Should the government continue its current policies, the tide of criticism will run even higher. Along with this will come a progressive cynicism toward even small levels of increases in defense spending. The government will have to work hard just to maintain the status quo. In this vein, Erik Nielsen only recently lamented that "It is surprising the number of Canadians who believe we won't have to defend ourselves." Thus, in addition to a sustained attack by those who want to see Canada relieved of all collective security roles, the Conservatives will find themselves having to defend the country's weakened military posture against charges that Canada is neglecting its own and allied security interests—and this on top of greater public indifference.

This is only the internal criticism. Even if the allies accept whatever Canada has to offer, the lagging Canadian contribution will surely elicit greater criticism from abroad. This may not result in the imposition of penalties, but in subtle ways Ottawa may find its seat at the table increasingly uncomfortable. Certainly this will be the case for Canada's senior soldiers, sailors, and airforce personnel. Compared to the benefits that would flow from restructuring, the cost of continuing the present course seems insupportable.

Canada cannot change its unique position in the Western alliance in whose continued existence it has an abiding interest, but it has special responsibilities in North America that are not shared by the European allies, and its relationship to the West's security situation in Europe is only marginally comparable to that of the United States. Under more favorable international circumstances, Canada's position as the odd man out could be discounted or ignored. But with new challenges to both NATO and NORAD, it is time to exploit that Canadian uniqueness for Canada's benefit and for the benefit of its allies.

Notes

1. John W. Holmes, "Odd Man out in the Atlantic Community," in Holmes, *Canada: A Middle-Aged Power* (Toronto: McClelland and Stewart, 1976), 129.

2. Gerald Porter, *In Retreat: The Canadian Forces in the Trudeau Years* (Toronto: Denau and Greenberg, 1979), 28.

3. Transcript of a radio interview, August 1984; text courtesy of Progressive Conservative Party of Canada. Actually, the Leopard tanks are not 28 years old, but many of Canada's ships and aircraft are.

4. Canada, Secretary of State for External Affairs, *Competitiveness and Security: Directions for Canada's International Relations* (Ottawa, May 1985), 37–39.

5. *Calgary Herald*, April 24, 1985.

6. *Maclean's*, March 4, 1985.

7. *Maclean's*, March 18, 1985, p. 14.

8. *Canada's Defence Policy: Capabilities versus Commitments* (Ottawa: Business Council on National Issues, September 1984).

9. *Competitiveness and Security*, 37–38.

10. Henry A. Kissinger, *White House Years* (Boston, Mass.: Little Brown, 1979), 383.

11. Dean Acheson, "Canada: Stern Daughter of the Voice of God," in Livingston Merchant, ed., *Neighbors Taken for Granted: Canada and the United States* (New York: Praeger, 1966), 134.

12. William Epstein, "Canada's Disarmament Initiatives," *International Perspectives* (March/April 1979), 8.

13. *Toronto Star*, November 13, 1984.

14. John English and Norman Hilmer, "Canada's Alliances," *Revue internationale d'histoire militaire*, Edition canadienne, no. 51 (1982): 36.

15. John G. H. Halstead, "Canada's Security in the 1980s: Options and Pitfalls," *Behind the Headlines* 41, no. 1 (1983): 12.

16. Ibid.

17. John W. Holmes, *The Shaping of Peace: Canada and the Search for World Order*, vol. 2 (Toronto: University of Toronto Press, 1982), 29.

18. Quoted in Peter C. Newman, *True North, NOT Strong and Free* (Toronto: McClelland and Stewart, 1983), 56.

19. David Cox, "Defence Procurement, Defence Budgets, and Canada's European Defence Commitments," paper presented to Conference on Arms Control, Disarmament and Defence Policy: "Assessing Canada's Role in the 1980s," Queen's University, Kingston, Ontario, November 22, 1984.

20. Canada, Senate, Special Committee on National Defence, *Canada's Territorial Air Defence* (Ottawa, 1985), 16.

21. Charles T. Kamps, Jr., "Nordkapp: World War III in the Arctic Circle," *Strategy and Tactics*, no. 94 (Fall 1983): 16.

22. Erling Bjøl, *Nordic Security*, Adelphi Paper no. 181 (London: International Institute for Strategic Studies, 1983), 26–27. Bjøl does note that the U.S. military did not object strongly, believing that U.S. equipment might be vulnerable in the North.

23. Lieutenant General Charles H. Belzile, "Concentration and Deployment: The Canadian Air-Sea Transportable Brigade Group," *NATO's Sixteen Nations*, Special edition (January 1985), 21.

24. Canada, Senate, Committee on Foreign Affairs, Subcommittee on National Defence, *Hearings*, April 17, 1984, p. 8A:12.

25. U.S. Congress, Congressional Budget Office, *Shaping the General Purpose Navy of the 80s: Issues for FYs 1981–1985* (January 1980), xvii.

26. *Competitiveness and Security*, 13.